What People are Saying about *31 Days to Great Sex*

"Sheila packs months' worth of encouragement into this handy *31* guide! Get ready to turn up the heat in your marriage and sizzle in the bedroom!"

Shannon Ethridge,
Speaker, Life/Relationship Coach, and Author of the best-selling Every Woman's Battle Series

"I love the practical nature of *31 Days to Great Sex*. It's one thing to tell a couple to grow in intimacy. It's another to explain just how that is done. With a month's worth of encouragement and fun challenges, Sheila takes the mystery out of the journey."

Lori Byerley
The-Generous-Wife.com

"Want remarkable sex in your marriage? Sheila understands what it takes and is ready to share her relevant insights with you. This book is like having a conversation with a good friend!"

Julie Sibert
Speaker and writer at www.IntimacyInMarriage.com

"You may want better sexual intimacy in your marriage, but how do you achieve that? Sheila Gregoire's *31 Days to Great Sex* provides a month of daily challenges that profoundly and practically guide couples from ho-hum to humming in the bedroom!"

"J"
Blogger at HotHolyHumorous.com

"This is one of the best eBooks on the topic!"

Noel Meador
Executive Director, Stronger Families
(Response to the eBook version)

31 DAYS to great SEX

Sheila Wray Gregoire

Love. Friendship. Fun.

31 Days to Great Sex

ISBN: 978-1-4866-0194-3

Printed in Canada.

Word Alive Press
131 Cordite Road, Winnipeg, MB R3W 1S1
www.wordalivepress.ca

Cataloguing in Publication information may be obtained through Library and Archives Canada

Contents

Introduction

Who doesn't want great sex?

To feel swept off your feet, to feel totally one with another person, to feel physical ecstasy—that sounds heavenly!

But not all of us experience that when we make love with our spouses. Some of us don't feel very much pleasure. Some of us have really low sex drives. Some of us feel rejected because our spouse doesn't seem to want sex very often.

No matter where you're coming from, I'm glad you've decided to launch into *31 Days to Great Sex*. This book is intended for married couples who want to experience real intimacy and ecstasy in the bedroom.

The month starts with a week of challenges designed to help us see sex in a more positive light, and then turns to challenges relating to the three aspects of intimacy: emotional intimacy in the bedroom, physical intimacy in the bedroom, and spiritual intimacy in the bedroom. As you move through the thirty-one days, more and more of the challenges have to do with sexual technique and spicing things up. But not all of them do. At the end, you'll find a week devoted to making sure the momentum keeps up, even when the challenges are over.

If you're eager to jump into the "steamy" stuff, please don't. Do the challenges in order. Our biggest sex organ is the brain. We need to think and feel the right things about sex before our bodies will work properly when it comes to sex. So often our biggest roadblocks aren't technique but communication. One of your biggest breakthroughs this month may be finally having the chance to really talk about important things.

How does it work? Each day has a new topic and a new challenge. Do the challenges! Actually putting principles into practice is far more effective than just reading about them.

Included in the book are three big "timeouts." Sometimes couples need a little bit of encouragement and time to process what they're learning, so it's okay if you can't get through the whole book in one thirty-one-day calendar month. Just work at your own pace. In fact, for many couples working through this series, sex has become a huge source of conflict, fear, and hurt. Some of the challenges may feel like you're ripping a scab off of a wound, so you may need those timeouts to reevaluate, take stock, and keep going.

Note, too, that many of the challenges don't actually involve making love. Many of them involve talking or sorting out big issues. While you'll definitely have fireworks this month, often one of the barriers to those fireworks is that you've never actually sat down and discussed what you want your sex life to be like, or what you enjoy, or what makes you nervous. Taking this opportunity to open those lines of communication will make the physical side of your relationship that much better.

You'll get the most out of these thirty-one days if you approach the challenges by asking, "What can I do to make my marriage better?" rather than thinking, "I really hope my spouse is listening to this so that they will change!" Instead of focusing on where your spouse is failing, look at what you can do to fuel intimacy in your marriage.

Finally, if you want to take a break while she's having her period, that's fine, too—although many of the challenges don't need to involve intercourse. So play it by ear. There are no hard and fast rules.

Sex is the number one thing that couples fight over. It's tied up in our identity, our feelings of self-worth, and our confidence in our marriage. It has the potential to either break you apart or bring you closer than you ever thought you could be. My dream and prayer for each couple reading this is that you will achieve the latter: that you will feel closer, that you will feel truly intimate, that you will feel one. Let's launch in!

Days 1–8:

Turning Sex into Something Positive

Day One: Catching the Vision

The Act of Marriage

Sex is everywhere. It's used to sell cars. It's used to sell movies. It motivates clothing purchases, vacation destinations, and even car choices. You can't get away from it.

But what is sex really supposed to be about?

When I was thinking about that question, I browsed the internet for a picture to match the blog post I would write (for this book began as a series of posts on my blog, www.tolovehonorandvacuum.com). I came across a picture of a man and woman in their wedding attire: she in a flowing white gown, he in a tuxedo. And they were sitting together on a bed.

I don't know how many of us would have been gutsy enough to have a wedding photograph taken on a bed (or how many of us would hang such a picture on our wall), but I think it's refreshing, because it says, "This is important. This is a vital part of our relationship. And it all starts now—after the wedding."

Sex is the physical acting out of everything that marriage is. We become vulnerable with one another. We become completely naked with one another—and that means real intimacy, not just physical intimacy. We cherish each other. We protect each other. But we also have a ton of fun with each other!

Think about it: in marriage, we are fully committed to one another for life. We love each other. We laugh together and cry together. In sex, we also do all of those things and express all of those things, because sex is uniquely created for that. God made sex to feel great, but He also made it to be a deeply intimate experience.

But while sex is supposed to be stupendous, what if that's not what you're experiencing? I read this on Twitter recently:

> Satan's big marriage strategy: get people to have sex before they're married. Then get them to stop once they're married!

Now, perhaps you don't believe in Satan—or even in God. That's okay. You can still get everything out of these challenges. But hear me out for a second. Here's the problem with so many of us having sex before we're committed for life. When sex doesn't involve commitment, it isn't about an emotional connection, or a spiritual connection, because there's no promise. It becomes only about physical pleasure. When that happens, sex can lose its ability to really cement us together in other ways.

The problem doesn't stop there. When we do finally get married and commit to someone, we often stop having sex. Or at least we have it rather infrequently. In surveys I took for my book, *The Good Girl's Guide to Great Sex*, I found that forty percent of couples made love less than once a week. We're just not connecting that often.

So the "act of marriage," which can be so wonderful, so fun, and so significant, often isn't even happening.

Or maybe for you it *is* happening, but it just doesn't feel very pleasurable. You can't figure out what all the fuss is about, and you're worried that it was created for everyone but you. Or you're haunted by your past—maybe stuff that you did breathlessly in the backseat of a car, or something that was done to you by an uncle, or a babysitter, or a date. Or maybe you have a hard time staying "present" when you make love, because you're haunted by images of porn, or movies, or TV shows. Maybe the intimacy is absent.

This month, we're going to walk through these issues and uncover ways to find the true freedom that sex is supposed to bring! Sex is supposed to be wonderful in three ways:

- Physically—we're supposed to feel wonderful together.
- Emotionally—we're supposed to be able to laugh, have fun, and develop a deep friendship.
- Spiritually—we're supposed to feel deeply intimate.

For the first week or so, we're going to start unpacking how we can increase the connection and laughter during sex, and then we're going to look at specific strategies to make sex itself great.

Great Sex Challenge—Day One

Challenge for Her:

On a scale of 1–10 (with 10 being the best), our sex life is:
Physically _______
Spiritually _______
Emotionally _______

Say this as a prayer, or just journal it if you're not religious:

- I believe sex was created to feel great physically, and that I'm supposed to have a sex drive and feel aroused, even if I don't feel that way right now.
- I believe sex was created to make me feel loved.
- I believe sex was created to make me feel at one with my husband.

Challenge for Him:

On a scale of 1–10 (with 10 being the best), our sex life is:
Physically _______
Spiritually _______
Emotionally ________

Say this as a prayer, or just journal it if you're not religious:

- I believe sex was created to feel great physically, not just for me but also for my wife. I believe God wants me to help her achieve that!
- I believe sex was created to make me feel loved and cherished.
- I believe sex was created to make me feel at one with my wife.

Wrap-Up Together:

Share with each other how you each rated your sex lives. Remember that it isn't a bad thing if you have big discrepancies; you're launching into thirty-one days together during which you're going to grow closer and learn more about making this area of your life great. It's important to start by taking stock, but give each other grace, knowing that you both are aiming to grow. If you're both heading in the same direction and are committed to the same goal, it doesn't really matter if you don't start at the same place!

Now talk to each other about what a great sex life in each of these three areas would look like for you. Be practical. What are you aiming for? What would you both like? You don't have to understand how you're going to get there yet. That will come! The important thing is that you see that is the way it was meant to be—that it was meant to be that way for you, too.

Whether you have major hang-ups, hurts, fears, or doubts, or whether things are just mediocre, sex is supposed to be a big positive in your life and in your marriage. See it. Picture it. Believe it! If we can start having a positive and excited attitude about sex, sex will likely improve astronomically.

Over the next month, we'll look practically at how we're going to make it a reality.

Day Two: Challenging the Lies

Sex may be a beautiful thing, but that doesn't mean that we all feel wonderfully about it.

What do you do if you don't have a positive attitude about sex? What do you do if you're bringing baggage into your marriage which makes it difficult to get excited about sex? Or what do you do if sex has just never felt that great, and you've almost given up? Or if it seems impersonal and solely physical?

No matter where you're at today, your sex life can start fresh. But sometimes that fresh start is endangered because we believe things that aren't true. As we're going to learn throughout this month, our primary sex organ is the brain. What we think about sex determines whether or not we enjoy sex, or whether we're able to experience deep intimacy when we make love. So here's your challenge for today: we're going to confront any lies you believe about sex, and replace them with truth.

Some of these truths come from a Christian perspective. If that's not where you're coming from, you can skip over them. But I'd encourage you to read them, because we all need some assurance that we don't have to live with guilt and shame.

1. You are a new creation. Are you haunted by things you did before you were married? Do you have flashbacks from old boyfriends or girlfriends? Or even ex-spouses? Are you bothered by past porn use?

All of these things can intrude on your ability to think of sex as something sacred between you and your spouse. When you start to have doubts, when thoughts of your old lovers start coming back, think about this verse instead:

> Therefore, if anyone is in Christ, he [or she] is a new creation. The old has passed away; behold, the new has come! (2 Corinthians 5:17)

You are a new creation. You don't have to be that old person anymore, and that old person no longer has a claim on you.

Perhaps you don't have much use for the Christian idea of being a new creation, but you obviously do believe in marriage, because you walked down that aisle. When we marry, we start fresh. You are now one flesh with your spouse, not with anyone else. The two of you, together, are *also* a new creation.

So when you have these negative thoughts, replace them with the positive: You are a new creation. You are one flesh. You were bought at a price.

2. You are pure. When God looks at you, He sees you as pure. Sometimes we have a hard time feeling like we're new creations because we know what we've done in the past. But other times we have difficulties because of *what was done to us*. We were abused, raped, fondled, or teased. And we feel like we're tainted, used, and dirty.

That's not the way God sees you. God doesn't judge you in terms of what others did to you; He only sees you in terms of what Jesus did for you. You are completely and utterly pure, once you believe in Him.

So the next time you start to feel dirty because of what was done to you, the next time you think that everyone else is healthy but you never will be, the next time you feel like there's no hope for you, remember this verse:

He will exult over you with loud singing. (Zephaniah 3:17)

Think of how you hold a baby and sing to it, so amazed at how new and precious it is. That's how God thinks of you. He rejoices over you! When you start having negative thoughts about your identity, replace it with that positive one.

3. You were created for pleasure. You were made to feel sexual pleasure. Men usually have an easier time believing this because they tend to be guaranteed pleasure when they make love. In fact, that's what usually ends a sexual encounter—when he reaches orgasm. But women were also created for pleasure, and I can prove it.

If you're a woman, you have a clitoris, a little knob of flesh just in front of your vagina, which has no other purpose in the body except to bring pleasure. Guys don't have that. Their primary sexual organs are multi-functional. That's not true for us. In fact, God put more nerve ends in the clitoris than he did in the entire penis! So God gave us a little piece of our bodies that was made simply to feel good—very good.

If you're a woman and sex isn't feeling great for you yet, you may have started to believe, "I will never have an orgasm. I can't see what all the fuss is about. Everyone else may like sex, but I never will." Stop it! Don't say those things to yourself. Instead say, "I was created to feel pleasure."

It's true. And wouldn't you rather say something true to yourself than a lie?

Some women reading this may not have experienced a lot of pleasure before. That's okay. In the surveys I took, I found that the best years for sexual pleasure for married women are between years sixteen to twenty. If you've only been married for a little while, then know this: women get more orgasmic with time and practice. So instead of doubting, worrying, giving up, get excited!

A word to the husbands: perhaps you've started to doubt whether your wife can ever feel pleasure. You, too, need to believe that she was created to feel pleasure, that her body is capable of it. You just need to learn how to get in the right frame of mind, nurture your relationship, and then move together physically. That may sound like a tall order, but it's a fun one. And it's not just possible; with the right frame of mind, it's probable!

4. You were created for intimacy. Not only were we created to feel wonderful during sex, we were created to feel intimate. Sex is supposed to unite us together not just with our genitals, but also our hearts.

Unfortunately, sex often becomes something which is more pornographic than intimate. When we think of sex, we think of something almost impersonal. What's sexy is the idea of what our bodies are doing, not the idea of who we're doing it with.

That's a function of living in our society. We've taken sex out of the context of marriage, so it's become only physical. Then, once you get married, it's hard to make that mental switch so that sex becomes something so much more. Pornography just adds to the confusion.

If you're wondering if you'll ever be able to feel love, and not just arousal, then repeat this to yourself: "I was created for intimacy."

Over the course of the month, I'm going to give you tools to experience that!

5. Sex is a beautiful thing. Sex is rather awkward. It's messy. You're all sweaty, and there's stuff to clean up afterwards. And sometimes it just doesn't seem, well, *proper*. It's easy for us to think sex is something we have to do to make babies, but perhaps it's really best not to dwell on it too much. Women, especially, like feeling in control. Clean and organized. Sex doesn't fit into that mold.

Maybe it's time to throw out the mold. Sex is supposed to be a little messy. Sex is supposed to make you vulnerable, a little out of control. It's not supposed to be clinical!

Some of us were raised to think that it was something never to be spoken of or thought of. Then, when we get married, that transition is really hard to make and we start to wonder if there really *is* something dirty or wrong with the whole thing.

That's another lie. I'm not saying you're bad for believing it; I'm just saying it's holding you back.

When God finished creating Adam and Eve, He pronounced them, naked as jay birds, "very good." Sex is very good. If you start doubting it, repeat that over and over, "Sex is beautiful. Sex is very good."

6. Sex benefits you. This is the most common one. Many of us have come to see sex as an obligation. When we think about sex, we tend to think, "Do I have to?" We figure we *should*, because our spouses need it. If you're the spouse with the lower libido, you probably have come to see sex as one more thing on your to-do list—hardly a sexy thought.

But sex helps you, too! If you're really tired, sex will help you get to sleep faster and sleep more deeply. If you're anxious, making love will help you calm down. Making love boosts your immunity, makes you less depressed, and best of all, it makes you feel more connected to your spouse.

Next time you think, "I guess I have to," stop yourself, and replace it with this: "Sex helps *me*."

I know many of you would like to move on to the nitty-gritty of sex. Don't worry: we're going to get there really soon! But before we can work at making the practicalities of sex work, we need to make sure we're believing the right things about sex. Sex isn't magically going to work if you're still walking around feeling dirty, embarrassed, guilty, or obligated. We need to get our heads in the game, because when our heads aren't there, our bodies won't follow.

Great Sex Challenge—Day Two

To Do Individually:

If you start to think negative things about sex, stop! Take those thoughts captive and tell yourself the truth instead. Repeat it if necessary. If you really want to make this challenge stick, journal some of the negative things you believe about sex, and then write the truth underneath. Sometimes just writing, thinking, and praying helps us to see our own negative thought patterns, and then reject them.

To Do Together:

Of all the lies discussed today, which do you have the most trouble defeating? Have you given up hope that sex will ever feel good for you—or for your spouse? Do you still feel like sex is a little creepy, or wrong? Do you see it mostly in pornographic rather than intimate terms? Talk about your roadblocks, and then talk about strategies you can work on together. That way, when you slip into the pattern of believing lies, your spouse can help you.

For instance, if your spouse has difficulty believing that sex can feel good, ask her (or him), when you start feeling hopeless, "What can I do to help redirect you? Can I hug you? You are created for pleasure, and one day we will get there, I promise." Or you can say, "You are beautiful to me. I love you and you are meant for so much more."

Alternatively, if he has trouble believing that one day he can feel like sex is intimate, rather than just pornographic, hug him and say, "You show me every day in little ways that you love me. You were created to love me in bed, and I know we will get there."

Talk about which affirmation would be most effective for the lies you each struggle with. Then start practicing them every day!

Day Three: Embracing the Skin She's In

Women, are you beautiful?

Just asking that question has probably laid a whole pile of guilt at your feet. You feel ugly. You feel too big. You don't measure up.

Guys, you may look at your wife and think she's beautiful, but I can practically guarantee that she doesn't think so. Everywhere she turns she sees images that she'll never be able to compete with. So she feels ugly, and when we women feel ugly, we feel distinctly unsexy. Today's challenge is going to be about helping her celebrate the skin she's in!

Let's look first at the root of the problem. Women have always wanted to "be the beauty," as John and Stasi Eldredge say in their book, *Captivating*.[1] Men tend to be the ones who pursue; women tend to be pursued. In order to feel sexy, there needs to be something about us that's worth pursuing! So beauty becomes important.

Add to that our culture's obsession with sex outside of a committed relationship, and beauty takes on even more of importance. When sex is taken outside marriage, all you have is physical attraction.

1 John and Stasi Eldredge, *Captivating* (Nashville, TN: Thomas Nelson, 2007).

"Sexiness" becomes of vital importance. Even if you're married and you value the other aspects of sex, our culture's obsession with sexiness still impacts us.

Picture in your mind the covers of *Maxim* and *Cosmo*, for instance. *Maxim* is for men and *Cosmo* is for women. *Maxim* may be black and *Cosmo* pink, but other than that they're pretty much the same. Both feature semi-naked women looking as if they're on the prowl. This ideal of super-sexed voluptuous females has taken over.

Most of us, however, don't look like that. In fact, supermodels don't even look like that. They're all airbrushed. And so all women go through life feeling inferior. When we don't feel sexy, it's hard to feel in the mood. Part of feeling sexy is feeling comfortable in our own skin, and many women are so embarrassed and ashamed of their own bodies that they do our utmost not to think about them. We hide them in oversized clothes. Anything that reminds us of our physical bodies also reminds us that we're inadequate. That's why we often become dissociated from our bodies. We don't want to feel fat.

One of the most frustrating things for my husband was when he would proposition me. I would reply, "I just don't feel attractive." His response: "If I want you, you are, by definition, attractive!" He was attracted to me. But I didn't feel attractive.

Note for women: Given that even supermodels are photoshopped, are we going to allow our culture to set our sexual self-esteem? Are we going to allow our culture to make us feel ugly, and thus rob us of the pleasure we're supposed to feel in marriage?

Ladies, if you're like me, you're tired of all the negative messages coming out of our media about how we should look. But if you're tired, then why not just say no? Tell yourself, "I will not let our culture dictate how I should think about my body. I was designed for pleasure—no matter what I look like—and I am going to feel it!"

Ironically, as you embrace your body and accept it, it actually becomes easier to take care of it and lose some of the extra weight. Women who have more self-confidence have an easier time shedding pounds than those who don't. If you're packing an extra sixty or eighty pounds, the answer isn't to berate yourself about it. It's to embrace the body you do have and have as much fun with it as you can. Love your body, and you'll treat it better.

Note for men: I receive many emails from women who say to me, "My husband is upset that my body doesn't look like it did before I had kids. He tells me that he's not attracted to me anymore. He doesn't want to hurt me, but he feels like he should be honest. But I just can't lose the weight. What do I do?"

Men, maybe your wife has gained some weight. She probably doesn't look like the women in movies or in magazines (although those women don't look like that, either). Here's your choice: you can further demoralize her and wreck her self-esteem, which will cause her to flee from sex even more, or you can embrace her, show her you love her, show her you want to have a great time with her, and boost her self-esteem.

Studies show that women who appreciate their bodies have a much easier time losing weight than women who feel lousy about their bodies. You are in a unique position to help your wife get over her insecurities and embrace her body. Will you do it?

Great Sex Challenge—Day Three

Challenge for Her:

Name the five features you like best about your body. You must name at least five! Three or four aren't good enough. All of us can name five things that we hate, so today name five that you love. And don't ask your husband to help!

Once you've come up with the five, share them with your husband, and ask him to give them some special attention. Then have some fun dressing up those parts of your body. Do you like your breasts? Stand naked in front of your husband, wearing nothing but a long, dangly necklace. Do you like your hips? Take some lipstick and draw a little heart tattoo to surprise your husband. Do you like your eyes? Put on some mascara. Have fun with your body. For the next week, tell yourself, over and over again, "I love my breasts. I love my eyes. I have amazing feet." Let's say something positive rather than something negative!

Challenge for Him:

Your wife is insecure. It doesn't matter if she looks like a supermodel to you or if she's packing an extra hundred pounds. She's insecure. All women are.

Today your goal is to help her feel beautiful, and that means you need to commit to letting her be the beauty in your life. Your eyes must be entirely for her. Like Proverbs says, *"Let her breasts fill you at all times with delight"* (Proverbs 5:19). This is directed at men who are married to women who are past their prime and who have nursed many babies. And it's a command!

Sure, lots of women are more attractive than your wife. But you are called to love your wife, not them. She needs you to find her beautiful. Desperately.

So tonight, tell her what five things you love most about her body (after she has revealed her own list). Touch them. Tell her what's so great about them. Show her that she makes you excited—even more excited than any supermodel. Caress her. Reassure her. Show her that she is sexy!

Day Four: Pucker Up!

Do you remember your preteen dreams of a first kiss? You watched all those after-school specials on TV and you could hardly wait until it happened to you. You pictured it. You practiced it in your mind. You imagined who it would be with. In those heady days when you were prepubescent, kissing was likely as far as those fantasies went.

Then, for so many couples, you got married and kissing almost came to a halt.

I think it's because of a misunderstanding of what kissing is for. Men, for instance, often think kissing is foreplay—as in, it's going somewhere. Because many women are reluctant to put a downpayment on something they may not want to purchase later, so to speak, they stop kissing, so that he doesn't get the wrong idea.

Kissing then becomes something that she may actually avoid unless you're about to have sex. And he may avoid it, too, thinking it's not really necessary except in the bedroom. That's too bad, because kissing actually makes us women feel closer to our men! It's fun, it's intimate, and it grosses out the kids (in a good way).

Just because you're not sure you're going to want to make love in the evening is no reason to avoid kissing earlier in the day (if a woman always turns her husband down, that's a problem, but we're going to get to that later). If a man avoids kissing, he deprives his wife of one of her primary ways of getting her libido up, almost guaranteeing she *won't* want to make love later.

Most couples only kiss today as foreplay, not throughout the day. If they do kiss, it's just a quick peck. So I want you to start kissing—really kissing—everyday!

Quick Kissing Tips

- Saliva. Some like it, others don't. Find out what preference your spouse has (and tell your spouse yours).
- Tongue. Same thing. Some really like it. Some don't. Keep it light! If your spouse is too tongue-happy, say, "Let me kiss you for thirty seconds and show you how I like it." And then do so enthusiastically!
- Breath mints are your friend. Have some in your purse and use them throughout the day. Toothbrushes are your friend, too!
- Use your hands. Caress your spouse's back, arms, head, or wherever you like!
- Savor it. Here's a tip for the guys: don't rush to turn kissing into something else. The romance of it will rev her engines. If you hurry things, and start groping her or touching her breasts every time she walks by, or slip your hand under her shirt every time you kiss, chances are you'll turn her off. Think of kissing like an amazing appetizer before a meal. You don't gorge it down so you can get to the meal; you enjoy it for itself. So just kiss her! It helps her feel loved and wanted.

Great Sex Challenge—Day Four

Set the kitchen timer and kiss for at least fifteen seconds straight. It's amazing how long fifteen seconds actually seems. Start repeating this everyday, during the day (not just at night while you're lying in bed). You'll find yourself feeling more warmly towards your spouse, and sex will feel a lot more intimate.

Day Five: Awaken Her Body

When I wrote this study, I decided that I should work on it, too. I have to admit that Day Three was a challenge for me. I decided that if I was going to challenge women to name five things they like about their bodies, I should play along. So I sat in bed with my husband and tried to come up with five. It was surprisingly hard! Naming five things I hate is easy, but what was I actually proud of?

Many women just don't like our bodies, and because of that we're often disconnected from them. And if we're disconnected from our bodies, we aren't going to feel a whole lot of pleasure. That disconnect could be because we feel embarrassed about our bodies, or embarrassed about sex in general. It could be because as a couple you have never really figured out how to make sex feel good. It could be because she's starting to doubt whether she actually *can* feel good.

Today we're going to focus on reassuring *her* that her body can indeed feel pleasure, and showing *him* that he can actually provide that. While in movies people may grope each other and then fall into bed in rapturous pleasure automatically, most women don't work that way. They take far more time. On the big screen, arousal is instantaneous, making women start to worry that there's something wrong if two minutes of ripping off clothes isn't enough to arouse them. Men may start to wonder if their wives actually enjoy sex at all.

For those of you who have seen *The Notebook*, you'll know that Allie, who's a virgin, has mind-blowing sex her first time out of the gate. She makes mad, passionate love with Noah, and everything goes so amazingly wonderfully. She orgasms. She feels great.

Women watch that sort of thing and think, *That's what sex is like for everyone but me. I'm a freak. I have to work so hard to feel aroused, and I'm not even sure I can get aroused. It will never work for me.* And men watch that and may think, *What's wrong with my wife? Why doesn't she respond like that?*

Hold it right there.

Remember Day Two, when we talked about some of the lies we believe? One of the most common lies for women is, "I will never feel pleasure." It's not true.

Women were made with body parts specifically designed to feel pleasure—and we're going to talk about the clitoris more throughout the month. But just because women have that little body part doesn't mean it gets stimulated enough in a few minutes to make sex wonderful. Movies aren't an accurate representation of reality.

Instead, here's what happens with so many couples. He fumbles a bit trying to make her feel good, but he may not know the right way to touch her, because men and women like to be touched differently. Men like a firm touch; women like it much more lightly. If a man touches a woman the way he wants to be touched, it's not going to be pleasurable.

So he does that, and she's too embarrassed to speak up. She thinks, *I guess I just don't like my breasts touched*, or *I guess I'm just not sensitive*. She gets increasingly anxious about why she's not feeling pleasure, so she tries to force herself. That makes it even worse, because when we're anxious, we can't relax, and when we can't relax, we won't feel very good.

Are you in that vicious circle? Maybe you're not, and you're here for tips on how to make sex even more wonderful. It's okay right now, but you'd like to ramp it up. That's wonderful, and I think you'll get a lot out of this month! Other couples, though, are having some serious problems in the bedroom, and going through these thirty-one days may be a difficult process.

I received this email when I was working through this series on my blog:

> Sex has long been a really, really hard part of my marriage. No matter what we've tried, it's not getting better. It's worse. Yesterday's blog post about lies was painful. It felt like you'd listened in on my internal monologue and aired it to everyone. I was really upset—and thankful.
>
> I might have to make cue cards to remind me of the truths you shared.
>
> I asked hubby to do this series with me. He jumped at the chance, because he knows how much of a struggle this is with me. And tonight we started.
>
> Wow. We haven't talked like that in so long. It was amazing.
>
> Although we have a long way to go, thank you for making it possible for us to open the lines of communication.
>
> Tonight, I want to cry because I feel like maybe, just maybe, there's hope I'll become the woman God intends me to be, the woman my husband prayed for, the woman I should be.
>
> By the way, I couldn't think of five. My husband suggested some of his top parts, but I had a hard time accepting them. I really did. I could only come up with one, and that was a hard one to think of. It's much easier to like the inside me. The outside me—I don't know how. But thank you for making me think of it, to start looking at myself.

I'm so glad that she feels like they're finally able to communicate, and that there may be light at the end of the tunnel. Today I want to give you a challenge that will give you both even more confidence and encouragement.

Great Sex Challenge—Day Five

Light some candles, get a space heater to make sure your bedroom is comfortable, and put some massage oil on the bed. Now take a timer and set it for fifteen minutes. For the next fifteen minutes, while she lies still, he will explore her body, without any expectation that she will actually orgasm. And you can't make love! This isn't foreplay. This is just *play*. He can touch her wherever he wants.

Challenge for Her:

- If he's doing it too roughly, tell him gently (or take his hand and show him how to do it better).
- If it honestly gives you the willies (if you have anxiety from previous abuse, for instance), you can ask him to move on to a different body part—but you must let him keep touching you!
- Do your utmost to concentrate on what he's doing. Don't worry about the timer. Don't worry that he's grossed out, that he doesn't want to do this, or that he thinks this is silly. Instead, I want you to think specifically about what he's doing. Pay attention to your body. Start asking yourself, "What wants to be touched now?" That may sound silly, but I'm asking you to do it not to issue him a report card. Instead, it's because if you ask yourself this question, you'll start paying attention to what your body is feeling. You may just realize you *do* want to be touched!
- Don't worry about having an orgasm! Honestly. Sometimes the reason we can't experience pleasure is that we get too goal-oriented. Just relax and treat it like a gift.
- Since he's probably going to be pretty worked up afterwards, you can always make love "for him," if you'd like. Get on top and give him a gift where he doesn't have to worry about you feeling good. The purpose here is to get away from anything goal-oriented and just learn that your body can, indeed, feel something. That's easier to do when there's no pressure and when you're relaxed!

- It could be that you're really nervous, and you have a hard time relaxing during those fifteen minutes. Try it in the bathtub if that's easier. And if this first time doesn't go well, don't fret. You may need to repeat this exercise a few times before you start feeling good. Use lots of massage oil and encourage your husband to concentrate on your legs and back, too, only slowly working his way to your more traditional erogenous zones. The goal is to learn to relax and to learn to just *feel.* If that takes a couple of sessions, that really is okay.

Challenge for Him:

- Start slowly. Don't go straight for her breasts or her clitoris. Rub her back, or the backs of her thighs. It's usually much more arousing if you build up to something than if you launch straight in, especially if she's nervous.
- Don't let her turn this into something for you! If she's nervous about feeling good, or about getting all this attention, she may try to say, "That's enough, now let's make love!" Don't give in. Give her the full fifteen minutes. Many women are embarrassed or scared to truly feel their bodies. Give your wife this gift.
- This is the hardest part. Agree in your heart and mind before you start that tonight may not go anywhere else. Yes, she may want to make love afterwards, but the best gift you can give her is to say, "There are no expectations. I want this night to be for you." Then touch her without expecting or demanding anything else. For so many women, sex has become an obligation, and that's not sexy. The purpose of this exercise is to help her see that her body can actually experience pleasure. If you turn this into an obligation, you risk this lesson (if she decides to do something else, of course, that's fine, but don't expect it). And don't worry: your turn is coming! Let tonight be her gift and her awakening, even if it's frustrating for you.

Day Six: Appreciate His Body

We've been looking at how to help her feel sexy, since she can't feel sexual if she doesn't feel sexy. But what about him?

Body image doesn't have quite the hold on men as it does on women, but it still matters. Many men naturally wonder if their wives find them attractive at all, especially if their wives have lower sex drives than they do. They may wonder, *Does she really want me?*

A note to wives: Maybe his body has changed. He made your knees wobbly when you married him, but the years have taken their toll. Now it's hard to look at him and say, "Hubba hubba!" He senses this. He's worried about it, too.

Certainly women are held to a ridiculous standard of beauty, but increasingly so are men. We watch movies like the Bourne trilogy, where a great-looking guy with major muscles can take out any bad guy with a simple chop to the neck. Our guy, on the other hand, is sitting beside us on the couch, watching the movie while balancing a bowl of chips on his beer belly.

Look, ladies, if we're going to complain about how women always feel like we have to live up to a crazy ideal, then let's not ask the same of our men! Watch where your eyes go. I've seen many married women on Pinterest, for instance, who keep a board of "eye candy," or good-looking male stars. That isn't acceptable. You're married, and you should rejoice in your husband, not in anyone else.

Maybe your husband is a little heavier now, and he isn't in the same shape as he was when you walked down the aisle towards him. Over the time you've had together, you've also shared memories, intimacies, and confidences. You've built a life together. Sex is more than physical; it also unites us emotionally and spiritually. Let's concentrate on that amazing connection, and maybe the fact that he's gained some weight won't matter so much.

A commenter on my blog mentioned that sex was really a challenge because her husband was heavy, and she didn't like feeling like she was suffocating. Very good point. If your husband is heavy, try being on top! That gives you more control, so you can line up the position better and hopefully find it more pleasurable (more on that later this month).

Remember, too, that even in marriages where the husband keeps a rock solid body, that infatuation feeling does fade. We won't always feel weak-kneed at our husbands. What becomes attractive and sexy doesn't need to be six pack abs; it could simply be that you know he loves you and protects you, and that he spends time figuring out how to make you feel good. A lover who is interested in making you feel pleasure is much better than one who may look awesome but doesn't learn how your body works.

So spend some time tracing his body, but encourage him to trace yours, too. Let him figure out how you work (and maybe you need to figure that out yourself). If he can learn to play you like a violin, the extra weight won't really be such a big deal!

A note to husbands: Sex is more than physical; it unites us emotionally and spiritually, too. Women are far more emotionally tuned into sex than they are visually tuned into sex. They really do approach sex differently than most men do. If you have a close relationship, usually the libido still falls into place.

Nevertheless, there are some things you can do to help. Both spouses owe it to the other to work on their appearance. If your body belongs to your wife, and hers to you, then you should be keeping it in good shape. So watch what you eat, and get out and get moving, even if it's only taking a walk after dinner. Packing an extra forty pounds is one thing; packing an extra 120 is another. You can still have a good sex life, but the loving thing to do, for both of you, is to treat your body well.

Also, present your body nicely to your wife. You may enjoy her wearing lingerie, but her biggest turn-on may be soap. Or toothpaste. So make it a habit of jumping in the shower after a long day at work, or brushing your teeth well before bed.

Finally, like I said to the women, what really makes a man a good lover is how he treats his wife in bed, not what his abs look like. It doesn't matter what your body is like; you can still make her feel wonderful. So set that as your goal! If you're on the heavier side, make sure you hold your weight on your forearms if you're on top, or that you encourage her to be on top. And when you do make love, use lots of foreplay and get to know her body really well. Show her affection, and take time giving her pleasure. That's what will boost her libido!

Great Sex Challenge—Day Six

Ladies, share with your husband what you find sexy about him. A few days ago, you had to name five things you loved about your own body. Now name five sexy things about your hubby. They don't all need to be physical (I find my husband's job kinda sexy, and I find his voice sexy), but come up with five things—and *some* should be physical! Share them your hubby, and then explore his body and make him believe it.

Day Seven: Understanding Each Other's Sexual Drives

Libido differences are the biggest source of conflict when it comes to sex. One spouse wants sex more than the other. Then one spouse starts to feel like they're begging, and the other spouse starts to feel like sex has become an obligation.

Usually it's the woman who feels like sex is an obligation, and the man who feels like he's begging. But that's not always the case. In the surveys I did for *The Good Girl's Guide to Great Sex*, I found that in about one-quarter of all marriages the woman actually has the higher sex drive. She's the one who's begging.

Today we're going to try to put ourselves in the shoes of the higher libido spouse and understand why sex is so important to him or her. I'm going to speak in generalities here, as if it's the husband who wants sex more. If it's actually reversed for you, just switch around what I've written so it fits with your experience. I'm not trying to leave anyone out.

What happens when you're the lower libido spouse? Many women feel as if sex is an obligation. If only he didn't want it so much, all the problems would go away. But he's sex-obsessed, which always makes her feel guilty. And that's why sex becomes a problem.

If it's him with the lower libido, he may think, "Why is she always pressuring me? Does she think I'm not enough of a man for her? What's wrong with her, anyway?" We start defining the problem as *my spouse wants it too much.*

Let's try looking at it in a different way.

Here's how I often explain it: men make love to feel loved, while women need to feel loved to make love. It seems like a recipe for disaster! But perhaps it makes sense. For each of us to get our deepest needs met, we have to reach out to the other. It's one of God's primary vehicles through which marriage brings holiness; it teaches us to think about the other.

I think women have a tendency to think we are the superior sex, because we care about important things, like relationships, while men care about shallow things, like breasts. But let's not forget that this is the way men were made, and it is for a purpose. Men like to feel as if they can chase a woman and win her. It's part of their identity. When we don't let him "win" us, he starts to feel like there's something wrong with him.

So what do you do? Recognize that the circle works both ways. Yes, when you're tired and say no, he feels distant. That makes him avoid you, which makes you angry and guilty, which drives a wedge. But when you're tired and still say yes, he feels close to you. That makes him release oxytocin (the bonding hormone), which makes him feel lovey-dovey towards you. That helps you sleep well, and then the next day he's often much more affectionate.

If you long to feel close to your spouse, the power is in your hands. I think what many of us women want is for our husbands to love us and act all affectionate *even if* we don't make love, and in an ideal world perhaps they would be able to. But that's asking an awful lot of a guy. Sex is so tied up in his ability to feel loved that you're basically saying to him, "I want you to shower me with affection and love me completely even if I don't show you any love at all." That's rough.

So today's challenge is to change the way you look at sex. Let's stop:

- Thinking that our husbands (or wives, if they have the higher libido) are pathetic for wanting sex so much, because they were made that way.
- Thinking that life would be better if sex didn't interfere, because sex bonds us together. (There are even hormones for that!)
- Thinking that we are morally superior for liking to cuddle, because we need to recognize that we were simply made with different priorities.
- Thinking that he should make the first move and show us affection regardless of whether or not we have sex (because then we're setting up an unfair double standard).

We're going to reverse the exercise from Day Five. I asked the husband to touch his wife to show her that she could feel pleasure. Today I challenge the wife to make him lie still while she spends at least fifteen minutes feeling him and touching him, any way she wants to. Shower him with some sexual attention! He'll feel really loved!

But here's something else: she'll feel really powerful. Sometimes we women become passive in bed, letting him make most of the moves. Then we miss out and don't see what effect we can actually have on our guys! Take that fifteen minutes and look at how you can reduce him to a whimpering mess as he begs you for some release. That's power, girls. And that's how much he wants you.

At the end of those fifteen minutes, you can do whatever you like (or he may have some very definite ideas of something he'd like to do). But take the full time to just touch him, because men are often so worried about whether or not their wives feel pleasure that to have a sexual interlude dedicated simply to making them feel good takes the pressure off and puts them on Cloud Nine.

If it's the husband who has the lower libido, this can also be an important challenge, because it can help build your intimacy and help ignite his sex drive. Libido is largely a "use it or lose it" phenomenon.

The longer you go without sex, the harder it is to feel aroused. But the more we make love, the easier arousal becomes. Our bodies become accustomed to it. If your husband rarely wants sex, then spending time reawakening his body can start to rev those engines.

Great Sex Challenge—Day Seven

Ladies, explore your husband's body for fifteen minutes straight, without letting him move! Concentrate on how his body responds, on what he likes, and on the effect you have on him. Watch how he feels really loved during this—and try to start seeing that desire he has for you as a very positive thing.

Day Eight: Hitting the Reset Button on Your Sex Life

Do you need a reset button for your sex life?

The emphasis during the first week of our thirty-one-day challenge is to start seeing sex in a new way. Next week, we'll turn to how to have more fun as a couple, but this week we're laying down the fundamentals: becoming affectionate again, getting rid of the lies we believe, dealing with our insecurities, and seeing our spouses in a different light.

Sometimes, though, that's not enough. Some of us have trunkloads of sexual baggage—whether it's lies we've believed, abuse that we've suffered, or even things we've done that we're not proud of. Maybe you had some sexual partners before you were married, and you wish you could get them out of your head. Maybe one or both of you were into porn. Maybe you even have a hard time getting over what you know your spouse did before you were married.

Today we're going to symbolically hit the reset button on our sex lives. What went on before doesn't matter.

Embrace Your New Identity

In Genesis 2:24, God said, "*Therefore a man shall leave his father and his mother and hold fast to his wife, and they shall become one flesh.*" When you're married, you became something new. What happened before doesn't matter; you have a new identity together now.

This can be difficult to accept, especially if you've been really hurt sexually in the past through abuse. For many people, sex seems dirty, and seeing it as something beautiful and new seems insurmountable. But God doesn't want you to allow that person, or persons, to rob you of the abundant life and marriage He has prepared for you. He wants you to achieve healing! So, pray with your spouse that you can see sex as something very different today than it was then. Make an appointment to talk to a counselor or a pastor if this is a longstanding problem, because we aren't meant to deal with everything alone.

Forgive Each Other

Sometimes, though, our problems don't predate marriage. Maybe you messed up after you walked down the aisle. Perhaps it's as damaging as an affair, or perhaps it's dabbling in pornography. These things break trust horribly with a spouse, and make intimacy so much more difficult to obtain.

You must deal with these things honestly, and that includes putting some accountability in place. It's not enough to say, for instance, "I used to use porn a lot, but I promise not to again, just please don't tell anyone else about it." If you are truly sorry, you will get accountability.

We aren't meant to struggle through life alone. If you've been tempted by porn, or had an emotional affair—or an actual affair—you need a same-sex accountability partner. You don't have to tell everyone under the sun, but telling one person is a way to show your spouse that you're serious about moving on and changing.

Once you've done this, the ball is in your spouse's court. If your husband or wife has broken trust, at some point you will have to forgive, or you cannot move on. There really is nothing he or she can do to make it up to you. It's not fair, but that's how it is. And so Jesus asks, "Can you let me pay the price instead?" You will never achieve true intimacy until you also extend forgiveness. Once your spouse has set up accountability systems, it is up to you to forgive and move on.

Take Every Thought Captive

We don't have to entertain every thought that comes into our heads. 2 Corinthians 10:5 says, "*Take every thought captive to obey Christ.*" When you have a thought, take it out, examine it, and then dismiss it if it doesn't line up with truth.

If you're haunted by memories of abuse, reject those thoughts. If you're haunted by thoughts of what your spouse has done, throw them out, too. You don't have to rehash everything multiple times. That also means you don't need to know in detail everything your spouse did. Asking for specifics so that you have more vivid visual imagery isn't going to help, and it's also going to hurt your spouse as your spouse tries to move forward.

If the issue is that you're haunted by what your spouse may have done before you were married (or after you were married through an affair), it may help to affirm this truth: making love isn't a matter of understanding everything about sex; it's understanding everything about each other. It's about how two people work together. What you and your spouse have is unique and beautiful, and doesn't warrant being compared with anything else.

Even if your spouse was married previously, you need to remember that sex is not interchangeable. What you have is unique because you both are unique. That's a good thing! So don't focus on "did he enjoy it more before?" or "did she like it better with him?" Focus on, "We are unique and beautiful together."

Great Sex Challenge—Day Eight

Pray through your reset together. Ask for forgiveness if you need to, and offer forgiveness if you need to. Thank God that you are both new creations and "one flesh" now.

Here's the fun part. Have a special dinner where you commit to starting over. Then make your reset visible! Buy new bedding (or commit to buying new bedding soon if you're reading this at night). Change the position of the bed in your bedroom. Buy new candles or new pillows. Do something different so that you can see that you are different now.

It may even help to add some humor to the struggle, perhaps by getting a buzzer that you can hit whenever you bring up past hurts or baggage. Some board games have buzzers. Keep one in your bedside table. From now on, if you feel antsy, like you're being drawn back into old arguments or old suspicions or old hurts, dig out that buzzer and say, "I need to hit this reset button again!" Then hit it, shake it off, laugh, and start again.

Timeout One

The last few days have brought *big* challenges, and some of you probably have problems with them. When running this series on my blog, one woman left this comment after Day Seven:

> This one seems impossible for me. I have a history of abuse—guys forcing me to touch them—and so I have this aversion to touching my husband sexually. I enjoy sex, but I don't do much touching during it. Will I ever get through this?

Another woman emailed me, saying that she found it really scary to ask her husband to touch her for fifteen minutes. It meant being so vulnerable.

But there are others who have already experienced breakthroughs, like this woman:

> The kissing thing has been a big issue in our lives because my hubby had a lot of problems with his teeth, so we just did not do it. When he got his teeth worked on, we just were not doing it anymore. I always missed it, but any time I brought it up we ended up fighting. So I was a little nervous when the blog about kissing came up. But we did it and last night we kissed like we haven't kissed in years. I am about to start

> crying while I type this. It was so wonderful and I feel closer to my husband today than I have in forever. It just opened something up in me. And as a side note, it did lead to the first big O I have had in about six months. Thank you and I can't wait to see what is in store for the rest of the month.

Some of you working through these thirty-one days are just looking for a tune-up, a way to turn the knob up from nine to a ten. That's wonderful! But a lot of you have some major issues when it comes to sex, either because you've brought baggage into your marriage, or because marriage has given you baggage. It's the one area you fight about a lot, and it's just never clicked. Perhaps you find yourself really worried about whether you can get better.

That's why today I want to give you a timeout to get some perspective, relax, and take stock.

I firmly believe that what matters, as with most things in life, is not so much where we are but the direction in which we are going. If you've enjoyed a great sex life in the past, but right now you barely talk to each other and you're super busy, you're probably in worse shape than a woman who has never experienced an orgasm but who is enthusiastic about trying to work through any issues that are there and trying to connect with her husband. In the long run, the person with the right attitude and goals will come out better than the person who started in a better place but isn't putting in the effort to maintain anything.

The purpose during these thirty-one days isn't to compare yourself to anyone else. It's not to force yourself to achieve something. *It's instead simply to start moving in the right direction.* This is the fork in the road, and you've decided to walk along the road that will bring you closer to real intimacy. That doesn't mean you're going to arrive, nor do you have to! But you're going in that direction.

Here, then, are some things to remember to make this thirty-one-day challenge really work for you.

1. Don't be goal-oriented. Be direction-oriented. You want to feel more relaxed, more confident, and more positive about sex. Not *completely* relaxed, *completely* confident, or *completely* positive about sex. Don't put pressure on yourself. Just commit to keeping an open mind, a positive attitude, and an "I'll try anything once" spirit!

2. Adapt to fit your circumstances. After Day Seven, I told the woman who emailed about being abused in the past to change the challenge so that instead of sexually stimulating her husband, she just got used to enjoying feeling him naked, even if all she did was give him a massage. You know yourself best; if you have to adapt, adapt.

But do try to do the challenges, because what you'll find is that the way I've set them up, they're not intimidating. I'm not trying to get you to do a particular thing; I'm trying to urge you to explore. With the Day Seven challenge, for instance, the woman was the one in control, which is much less scary for many women with baggage. If she can be in control and she set the parameters, she may find it easier to enjoy herself.

One more thing: at some point this month, she's going to get her period. That may mean that you choose to forego the challenges over those days, or you can choose to keep reading and trying (not all of them, after all, involve intercourse). Whatever happens, don't fret about it. This isn't a race. You haven't fallen behind.

3. Be patient with your spouse. If your spouse isn't embracing this as much as you would like, or is acting nervous, be patient. You can't force intimacy. Many of us do have genuine baggage that holds us back. Gentleness is the best way to deal with that baggage. Exasperation or impatience often drives people further away.

If your spouse is struggling, keep reassuring him or her of your love and acceptance and dedication to making sure that you *both* feel intimacy in your marriage. You can start by showing patience now. So, yes, please try the challenges, but reassure your spouse that you can take your time, and that you can ease into it. Remember that marriage is a lifetime commitment. You have time to get this right.

If you're ready to go on to another challenge tonight, by all means start Day Nine. If you've been struggling, though, it may be a better idea to redo one of the previous ones—especially the touching ones—or just spend the night snuggling before you start something else!

Heads up: the next challenge includes some things to do during the day, so it may be best to read it together in the morning.

Days 9–12:

♡

Laughter (Emotional Intimacy)

Day Nine: Fourteen Ways to Play as a Couple

When my oldest daughter was eight, she asked what I wanted for Christmas. When I didn't mention any toys, she felt so sorry for me. "**Why don't you like to play anymore, Mommy?**"

That's a good question. Why do we stop playing? Maybe Polly Pockets and Barbies aren't your cup of tea, but laughing and giggling and joking should be—because it's good for the marriage, and the soul!

Up until now, we've been looking at some of the roadblocks to enjoying a good sex life, and for many of you this has brought up issues of low self-esteem and baggage from sexual pasts.

Before we get to more sexual challenges, I want to address something at the root of many of our marriage problems: we stop having fun together. When we stop having fun, marriage becomes so, well, *serious*.

It's ever so much easier to address problems in our marriages—whether they're related to sex, parenting, finances, time, or whatever—if we also find time to laugh together. A couple that laughs together is also a couple who enjoys being together, and who will have an easier time navigating the difficulties of marriage.

Today I want to present you with a list of fourteen ways to play together as a couple. These aren't necessarily sexual, although you can certainly put a sexual spin on them if you want to. Later in the week, we'll look at how to flirt together, but today I just want to focus on laughter—specifically, laughter inspired by physical fun. When we have physical fun together, the more sexual fun often follows.

Before you launch into these "play" ideas, set the mood. If you want to have fun with your spouse, make sure he or she is in the right frame of mind and knows there's something playful coming. Don't just spring something on your spouse when he or she is worried about work or otherwise preoccupied. Send texts throughout the day, kiss lots when you're home, and laugh plenty beforehand. Then go for it!

1. Have a water fight. When you do the dishes, flick some water at your spouse and see what happens! Or, to turn it up a notch, give each other water guns and go for it! (This may work better when it's not winter for those of us in the Great White North.)

2. Throw a snowball. If snow is plentiful, text your spouse to warn him or her to be on guard when he or she pulls in the driveway tonight. Then set up an ambush! You can ask the kids to join in the fun, too. Physical play doesn't have to exclude the kids, and having all of you laugh together is a great preview of what could happen later that night.

3. Wrestle. I often win wrestling matches with my husband, because we make a deal. I have to move my husband (if he's standing) or push him off the bed (if he's lying down). He's not allowed to use anything to stop me except his body and perhaps two fingers. I can do anything I want. Even with those concessions, I still can't move him most of the time. But he laughs so hard that he often loses. Sometimes I let him win quickly, though, because what hubby doesn't like to get his wife pinned down? We always have fun with it and it almost always leads to "other" things.

4. Pillow fight! Ambush your spouse on the way out of the bathroom with a pillow. Then run while he or she goes to get one to hit you back!

5. "Pie in the face." Eating chocolate cake tonight? Or making chocolate cake? Smear it on him—and be prepared for it to be returned.

6. Act out a scene from a movie. Speaking of movies, a friend of mine recommends acting out dancing scenes or romantic scenes from movies. She says, "Turn off the sound and have the two of you provide the audio. See what fun or sexy lines you can come up with!" Or take the approach that Steve Carrell and Tina Fey did in the movie *Date Night*: when you're out in public, watch a couple talking and make up dialogue for them, or come up with a funny scenario for what they're doing together. Just laugh!

7. Dance. Turn your kitchen or living room into a dance floor! Turn up the music and dip and swing to your heart's content! Even if you don't know what you're doing, moving together can lead to lots of laughs.

Watch some clips from *Dancing with the Stars*—now that's sexy!—and try to copy them.

8. Box. If you own a Wii system, try the boxing game. You'll raise your heart rate, and she may just be able to knock him out! Then try to wrestle in real life and see who really is stronger.

9. Hit the courts. Play squash, badminton, tennis, or another racquet sport. Make him play with his left hand (or right hand if he's left-handed) if he's a lot better (or make her play handicapped if she's awesome!).

10. Play Solitaire to the Death. You'll be slapping down those cards so hard you'll work up a sweat! The winner gets something of their choice. It could be something sexual, or something like getting out of doing the dishes, or getting to take a bath while the other puts the kids in bed.

11. Indoor volleyball—in the buff! Blow up some balloons and play volleyball over the bed, while you're nude!

12. Tickling contest. Who will cry uncle first?

13. Turn chores into a game. One of my followers on Facebook gave me this idea:

> When we change the sheets on the bed, we have a race to see who can finish putting the pillowcase on the pillow and get the pillow on the bed in its place first. We do things like hide the opponent's pillowcase, throw pillows downstairs, grab the opponent's pillow, yank the pillowcase off and toss it in the hall, lock each other in the bathroom, and wrestle each other for our own pillowcases which the other is hoarding, hiding, or trying to throw out the window. There's much laughter, much tickling, and much running through the house and acting like children. It's fun!

14. Food fight. Finally, there's the staple from the high school cafeteria: the food fight. If you're cooking with your hubby and you "accidentally" get flour on his nose, what will he do back? There's something about play fighting that often ends in an embrace, and isn't that most of the fun?

Great Sex Challenge—Day Nine

Play! Pick an item—and do it!

Heads up: the next challenge includes some things to do during the day, so it may be best to read it together in the morning.

Day Ten: Preparing for Sex throughout the Day

I hope you had fun yesterday going over fourteen ways to play as a couple! All of those things will make intimacy more natural. Now we've got ourselves thinking in the right direction, and laughing together to smooth over issues and increase goodwill. But what about actually getting in a frisky frame of mind?

For most men, that's not much of a challenge. You just start thinking about sex and you're ready to go!

For many women, though, the mere thought of sex isn't enough to rev our engines, especially if there are other things on our minds. That's why it's important to lay the groundwork so that when you're together at night, sex seems like an attractive proposition.

Today, I'm going to talk mostly to the wives, though I will have some special words of wisdom to the guys at the end. However, if you're a guy with a lower libido than your wife, I'd recommend reading through some of these and applying them to your life.

Getting in the right frame of mind doesn't mean you have to be actively thinking about sex throughout the day. No one wants to be trying to get excited while talking to the boss, or while taking toddlers out on a walk. That seems kind of, well, icky.

But there's more to being sexual than just thinking or fantasizing. There's also feeling comfortable in your own skin, feeling comfortable with your spouse, and getting rid of the roadblocks to enjoying sex tonight.

Here's a game plan to help you use your day well.

Prepare Your Body

I live in the Great White North, where there are two seasons: winter and construction. Winter is substantially longer, so many northern gals throw those razors away in the winter. What's the point in shaving when no one can see your legs anyway?

No one, that is, except your husband. Let's face it: how sexy are you going to feel with "man legs"? Honestly, it doesn't take that long to shave (if you don't, that really is okay). If you shave in summer and feel good about it, and then stop in the winter, how sexy do you think you'll feel when you're nude in the middle of January? There's something about shaving that can make you feel pretty and prepared. So don't let yourself get too hairy!

Make your body itself feel great. Shave and use lots of lotion to keep your skin soft and smooth. When you feel better in your skin, you'll enjoy feeling your skin against his skin far more.

Prepare Your Clothes

Kiss frump goodbye. Even if you're dedicated to modesty, you don't need to be dedicated to frumpy. Wear clothes that make you feel attractive and that flatter your shape—whatever shape that is! If you think it's impossible, start watching episodes of *What Not to Wear*. They can dress any body shape and the women always end up looking incredible. If you just don't have clothes that make you feel confident, then go buy some. It's better to have six outfits that make you feel amazing than to have fifty T-shirts and seven pairs of mom jeans that make you feel dowdy.

If you spend your day looking and feeling attractive, it will boost your confidence at night. And don't forget our Day Three Challenge: concentrate on those five areas of your body you're proud of. Don't think about the things you don't like about your body; think about the things you do.

I personally think I have nice feet. Feet may not normally be the first thing people think of when they think "pretty," but I like my feet. I'm going to make more of an effort to pamper my feet and put on some nice toenail polish, because it makes me feel prettier.

So dress your body attractively, and play up those features you love!

Note to the guys: You can boost your libido by feeling more attractive and more like a man, too! Try to ditch the sloppy T-shirts at night and buy some attractive pajamas. When you get home from work, especially if you work at an active job, head to the shower first and suds up and brush your teeth. When you're clean, she'll be more receptive, and you'll feel more like it, too.

Carve Out Some "Me" Time

One of the biggest impediments to female libido is exhaustion. When I took surveys of two thousand women for my book, *The Good Girl's Guide to Great Sex*, the number one thing women reported that was wrecking their sex lives was simply being tired. When we feel like everybody is hanging off of us and everything is on our plates, we're going to absolutely crave time to ourselves. And when do we take that time? When the kids are in bed, right when we could be being romantic with our husbands!

If you just need forty-five minutes on your own every day, find a way to build it into your routine. It honestly is okay to stick the kids in front of a video for forty-five minutes so you can work on a scrapbook page if you have to. It's more important to have a great marriage than it is to spend every waking minute stimulating your children. If you work outside the home, don't have lunch with co-workers if you can help it. If you need time just to read a novel, then read a novel.

Make a list of some things which help to center you and make you feel sane, whether it's doing a hobby for half an hour, reading a book, soaking in a bath, or going for a jog. Now figure out how you can make this a reality. If you can take time for yourself during the day, you really will be more rejuvenated at night.

If you just can't see where that time can come from, talk to your hubby and explain why you need it. Maybe he'll volunteer to put the kids in bed just so you can take a bubble bath!

Note to the guys: This is just as important if you have a high-stress job during the day. Try to resist the urge to bring work home, or, if you have to, put a time limit on it. And don't let that time limit be, "I'll stop at bedtime." Stop a good two hours before you plan to turn in with your wife, so that you have some time to decompress. One of the leading causes of low libidos is high stress. When you're stressed, you're not as productive. Carving out time to relax is key to your productivity at work, but also to your intimacy in marriage.

Plan Regular Times to Imagine Sex

Women don't tend to have biological cues that remind us about sex the way men do. Men are very visually oriented, so even if they don't mean to think about sex, when they see a pretty woman their minds often turn that way. If they haven't had sex in a while, their body actually feels it. Most women don't experience this.

You need a reminder, or a trigger, to think sexy! What about choosing one common activity, or one trigger point, that makes you smile or think about the last great encounter you had? Say, every time you do the dishes, you think about your favorite sexual memory. Or perhaps every time you're at a stop sign, or every time you hear a siren, you can even text your husband and say, "Remember when…" (Just remember not to text and drive!)

Sleep

This may not sound very exciting, but it's awfully important. Get some shuteye! Exhaustion is a big culprit in killing our libidos, so we have to treat sleep seriously. Most of us need at least eight hours of sleep. If the kids wake you up at 6:30, or if your alarm for work goes off at 6:30, you need to be getting to sleep at 10:30. That's *getting to sleep*—not crawling into bed and turning on the TV in your bedroom, or playing on Facebook, or even having sex. It means lights out—which also means you should be crawling into bed closer to 9:45 if you want to have some cuddle and talk and fun time with your spouse.

Great Sex Challenge—Day Ten

Challenge for Her:

Put all that together, and what do you have? Spend your morning making sure you feel attractive. Find some "me" time throughout the day. Think about sex, even if it's just fleeting, a few times throughout the day. Then make sure you get some sleep at night, so you don't collapse when you are together. That's a lot for one challenge, so I'd suggest that you pick one or two that you know will really help and decide to implement them tonight—or tomorrow.

Challenge for Him:

Feeling attractive and energetic are two keys to a woman's sex drive. If she feels frumpy and tired, it really doesn't matter how much she loves you; she likely will not feel overly sexy. Help her out! If she needs new clothes to make her feel pretty, make that a priority in your budget. Even just one or two outfits can make a huge difference. If she needs time to herself, help her figure out a way to get it.

Finally, prioritize sleep. Don't watch TV in your bedroom too late and keep her awake. And don't watch TV or play video games yourself until midnight, then hope she'll still be energetic. Think about making love as an early evening activity, if your work schedule allows it—or a morning activity, if necessary! Work together at helping her get rid of some roadblocks to making love, and you'll find you both feel more confident and intimate.

Day Eleven: Show Affection

Remember our fifteen-second kiss a day? I hope you're still smooching away! It's so important to help us feel connected.

Now, we've talked about how to play together, and how to think and prepare for sex throughout the day. Tomorrow we're going to relearn how to flirt! But before we get there, let's talk about affection.

For most men, sex is the need, and affection is the choice. For most women, affection is the need and sex is the choice.

Really think about that statement for a moment. Whichever one is your biggest need, realize that your spouse feels the need for the other with exactly the same intensity.

One of the problems in our culture is that affection has largely been separated from sex. Sex is no longer about a connection between two people as much as it is about a quest for an orgasm (not that there's anything wrong with orgasms). But it becomes about the body instead of the soul, the relationship, the love. For women, especially, that's a stretch. If sex in your marriage has become something tacked on at the end of a day after you didn't touch, didn't say sweet words to each other, and didn't laugh together, it can easily feel as if you're being used.

But women also need to understand that men may have difficulty showing affection when they don't feel loved. To a man, a big part of feeling loved is knowing that his wife desires him and wants him.

We're going to be working throughout this month on how to turn the notch up on our sex lives. But I think it's fitting to first turn the notch up on affection, because affection really conveys the message: *I cherish you*. Sex, then, isn't only about the joining of two bodies; it becomes about the joining of two hearts.

Here are some ideas for being more affectionate with one another:

1. Hold hands. Whenever you're walking with each other, or sitting beside each other, hold hands.

2. Touch. As you walk by each other, make it a habit to reach out and brush a shoulder, or pat an arm, or ruffle some hair. Especially if your spouse's love language is touch, it's so important to reach out and make that quick connection—a connection that isn't overtly sexual!

3. Say kind things. When my husband and I speak at marriage conferences, he tells the story of a couple who had been married for forty-five years. In desperation one day, the wife announced that they needed counseling. He was flabbergasted.

"Why?" he asked.

"You never talk to me. You never touch me. I don't even think you love me anymore."

He rolled his eyes. "Look, on our wedding day I told you that I loved you. If that ever changes, I will let you know."

Don't be like that guy. Make it a habit, every day, to tell your wife you love her.

And women, make it a habit, everyday, to tell your husband *why* you love him. Don't just say, "I love you." Say, "I appreciate so much how you provide for the family" or "The way you play with our son makes me so happy; he loves you so much" or "The way you handled that disagreement at church made me so proud to be your wife." Note the things that he does well, and tell him what those things are.

That's it. Just hold hands, touch, and say kind things. It's amazing how those three little things can change the whole atmosphere of a marriage!

Great Sex Challenge—Day Eleven

Hold hands while you talk through tonight's challenge. Talk about how doing these three things regularly will change the dynamic of your relationship. Share with each other two or three things that most attracted you to your spouse when you first met. What did you love about him? What did you love about her? Tell each other—in great detail!

Day Twelve: Flirt with Your Spouse!

When we're dating, we flirt. She winks at him. He takes her hand. She gives him that "come hither" look. But when we're married, too often we stop flirting. Why flirt when you've already got her? And if she flirts, she may worry that she'll give him the impression that she's definitely going to deliver tonight. You wouldn't want to promise anything like that.

Here's the problem with that strategy. Women's primary sex organs are their brains. For us to get in the mood, our brains have to be engaged. Take flirting out of the equation and you take away one of our primary tools for boosting our libidos! Feeling desired by our spouses is another big libido boost, as long as it's done in the right way.

We're one-third of the way through our thirty-one days to great sex, and a few days ago we looked at how to prepare your mind for sex throughout the day. We weren't looking at anything particularly frisky, just things to make you feel more at ease, more confident, and less tired.

Today we're going to turn it up a notch and learn to flirt! Just as playing together helps you laugh together, flirting helps you to bind together because you share a relationship with your spouse that is totally unique.

Here are some ideas to get the fun rolling.

1. Leave a love note on the mirror. Using a dry erase marker (or even lipstick), leave a love note on your honey's bathroom mirror. To be even bolder, draw a picture of what you want to do later.

2. Kiss in the car at stoplights. That never gets old. And don't forget at least one fifteen-second kiss a day!

3. Have a secret code phrase. Want to tell him you think he's hot? Try a secret code phrase, like "Are we due for an oil change?" No one else will know what you really mean but him, so you can say it in front of the kids, in front of your parents, in front of anybody!

4. Play the fortune cookie game. Whenever you get a fortune cookie, mentally add the words "in bed" to the end of it. You'll giggle together at a Chinese restaurant as you pass them to your husband, but no one else will know why you're laughing!

5. Grab some flesh. When he's walking by, smack his butt! Now, here's where things may differ for guys. If she's doing the dishes and you walk up behind her and squeeze her breasts, she's likely to get a little ticked off. Many women write to me, saying, "My husband is always grabbing me! It makes me feel so used!" Men may not mean it that way, and many men actually enjoy being grabbed. But women don't, at least not in the same way.

While women can be bolder, it's often better for men to start off with a lighter touch. Instead of grabbing her breast, stroke her shoulder. If you're sitting on the couch next to her, run your fingers through her hair. Hold her hand as often as you can. If she giggles and returns the attention, then by all means try something a little friskier!

6. Set up a cozy love nest for watching movies. Want to watch a flick tonight? Share pillows and a blanket and play footsie. One respondent on my survey for *The Good Girl's Guide to Great Sex* said that she and her husband had "topless movies" where they snuggled up under the blankets minus any tops. Tons of fun!

7. Wives, ask your husband to choose your panties for the day. Paul, from agenerousHusband.com, told me about this one. If he chooses them, he'll be picturing you in nothing but them—all day.

8. Leave sticky notes in unexpected places. Also from Paul: try to always use the same color, so he knows they're from you! If you're near her place of work during the day, stick a note under her windshield wiper. Get the waitress to put one on his plate when you're eating out. Get the kids in on it, too!

9. Text, text, text each other. Text about anything—song lyrics, memories of fun times you've had, what you're wearing, what you're thinking about, etc.

10. Stick notes in his lunch. One fan on my Facebook page shared this idea:

> I also write stuff on his brown bag lunch. For a while, I thought it might embarrass him. But when I stopped, he pouted. They aren't always "sexy." Some are just sweet. But tomorrow's lunch has written in red letters: "For My Red Hot Lover!" *grins*

11. Flirt in a crowd. Gina Parris, who writes at winningatromance.com, says you should try catching your husband's eye in a crowded room and wink at him. Pass him a note that says you're available and you think he's cute. Or walk up to her and try a cheesy pick-up line!

12. Flash him, but not in public. Gina Parris also told me:

> Yes, this is ridiculously forward, but if you do it while he's watching TV, and then just walk away, at least you will have raised his blood pressure—and raised your own sexual energy

for a greater chance of engaging in a little more fun.

One of the commenters on my blog also recommended doing chores vigorously—and bralessly—so he can appreciate the bounce! When you mop the floor, wear a skirt but go commando and get down on all fours to see if he notices.

13. Stick a surprise somewhere interesting. Another Facebook reader emailed me this tidbit:

> My husband recently got back from a long out of state trip. It was late when he got home but I was expecting him. He quickly showered and came to our room in new underwear (that was a color! something I had been longing for in a long time). He said "I have something for you." I thought it was the underwear and I commented on how nice they were between smooching. "No, I have a gift for you in them." I thought he was just being cheeky; of course he's a gift! So I reached in in, and there was a jewelry box! That was not what I expected! It was a sweet gift, and his creativity was so memorable! He has inspired my own games of hide and seek, may it be a note written with a wash-off marker under my panty line or some little item in my bra… it's a fun way to play every now and then.

14. Go commando. "J," who tries to remain anonymous at hotholyhumorous.com, is a big believer in this one! She suggests forgetting to don knickers under that dress or skirt for your date, then whisper to him in the restaurant what you're doing later that night.

15. Play "Strip" Anything. Turn any board game in your home into a sexy time by adding "strip" to the beginning: Strip Battleship (an item of clothing for each sunk ship), Strip Scrabble (for every word worth twenty to thirty points), Strip Monopoly (an item of clothing every time you pass Go or to get out of jail), etc.

16. Play footsie. When you're at a restaurant with tablecloths, slip your shoe off and let your toes explore his legs. Get him all worked up while you carry on a normal conversation!

Flirting Rules of Engagement for Her:

A few ground rules. When you flirt, you're telling your husband, "I'm interested. I find you attractive. I want you." So if you do add flirting into your relationship, you're going to have to make sure you add some sex in there, too, or else your guy is going to get very mixed messages (and he'll be very frustrated).

Does flirting mean you have to follow through each and every time? No, not necessarily. But allow me to let you in on a little insight. Men don't just want sex because it physically feels good. They want to feel wanted. Flirting is one of those ways that make them feel wanted, and if it's followed up by regular and frequent sex—say, a few times a week—most guys won't mind if you don't have sex every night, even if you did flirt. When men get regular and frequent sex, they become more secure and confident in the fact that you love them.

One of the reasons men often seem desperate for sex is because they're desperate to know that they actually are desired. It's not only the physical release they need; it's that emotional and even spiritual validation that says, "I value and want you." When they're getting that from you regularly, you have a lot more room to play, kiss, and flirt without necessarily having to make love right then and there. When you're not making love with your husband frequently and regularly, he'll be less able to let these little things go.

So if you're thinking, "Every time I kiss my husband he wants it to go somewhere" or "Every time I flirt he wants something else," it may be that your husband is insecure about whether you really want him, because sex is infrequent, or perhaps because you never initiate.

We're going to talk later this month about how to get you in the mood and how to make sex more fun and less stressful for you so that you desire it more often. But for right now, flirting is a fun way to play with your husband, to boost your own libido, to get you thinking along those lines, and to make your husband feel wanted. If flirting is combined with regular sex, you'll feel more confident in your relationship!

Flirting Rules of Engagement for Him:

Flirting is a ton of fun, but instead of thinking of flirting as a way to tell her you want to have sex, think of flirting as a way to communicate, "I love you. I value you. I think you're a ton of fun." Think of it as something to make you giggle together, rather than a prelude for something right away. It's an extension of the affection exercise we did yesterday, just turned up a notch.

I know that can be a tall order, but many women feel objectified, thinking you only want them for one thing. But to take flirting out of a marriage entirely also takes out a lot of the fun! So add affection, lots of touch, and lots of giggles. Then take your cues from her. If she gets racier, feel free to turn up the notch, too!

Great Sex Challenge—Day Twelve

Sprinkle these ideas into your lives until they become natural. And think of some of your own! Throw yourself into them. Have fun. If you get in a truly flirty frame of mind, you may find that your own libido goes up because the fun quotient in your marriage goes up.

Timeout Two

My plan for this month is to lay out a strategy to help you get the most out of your marriage. Why settle for mediocre when sex is a vital part of your relationship—one that God designed to bind you together, to give you great pleasure, and to add fun and sparks to your life?

This week is going to be a good one. We're going to explore (if that's the right word) how to make sex feel stupendous. When I published a version of this on my blog, right about now I started receiving plenty of emails from people who were just finding it too difficult. Many others, however, wrote saying that for the first time they felt like they were connecting.

Still others, though, wrote with basically no hope. How can anyone tell you sex can be good when it obviously is not?

I know many of you think this is hopeless. But please, hear me out: don't you wish it were different? Don't you wish sex could be good? Do you really want to live your life with so much distance between you? When you have children, you owe it to them to make sure your marriage is rock solid, and that includes having a close, intimate relationship with your spouse. One way you can do this is to try these things I'm suggesting with an open mind. Now, I'm not the answer to all your problems, and if you have a better way, that's fine. But please, try *something*.

If sex is a huge roadblock, that's okay. But please, imagine that it's not. Believe that it doesn't have to stay this way. Your main sex organ is your brain. What you think about sex will determine your arousal level, the pleasure you get from sex, and your attitude. So can you just try? Just take little baby steps?

If you go back to the beginning of these challenges, you'll find that's what I'm recommending—baby steps. Just little things, every day. It's a good place to start. Please don't give up. You were made for more than this. You were made to truly experience intimacy. You may not see how that can happen, but can you try?

Pray about your sex life, together if you can. Pray that God will give you His mind about sex and repair some of the lies, if you've believed any. If you don't think you've believed lies, but you just hate sex, then pray about it anyway and ask God to show you how things can be better, and where you may be sabotaging yourself.

Days 13–19:

♡

Making Sex Feel Wonderful (Physical Intimacy)

Day Thirteen: Getting Her Head in the Game

We've looked at how to reframe how to think about sex, how to reframe the way we think about our bodies and about pleasure, and even how to think of our spouses differently. We've looked at how to get in the right frame of mind during the day by flirting, playing, and preparing for the evening. Now we're going to turn to what to do when the evening finally arrives. Today, we're going to look at how to get her head in the game, and then we'll turn to foreplay, orgasm, and more!

Let me start with some basics that many men and women don't understand about the female libido: if her head isn't in the game, her body won't follow. If she's distracted by anything, it's difficult to get aroused. This is the exact opposite of men, whose bodies often react to visual stimuli even if they *are* distracted and don't want to be thinking about sex. Most men react almost automatically; women need to decide to react.

I've often heard it said that men are like microwaves and women are like slow cookers, insinuating that men can heat up and be done quickly, while women take more time. But I think that analogy is false because it implies that women will, eventually, heat up. The truth is there is no guarantee. A guy can do exactly the same thing to his wife that yesterday had her in raptures, and today he can tell she's lying there, thinking, *Will you just get it over with? I want to get to sleep.* While women certainly can heat up, men can't do it completely for us. We control the switch. We're the ones who need to decide to participate, and that's not always easy.

Consider this scenario:

> She walks into the bedroom to find her husband giving her that "Y'wanna?" look. She smiles and begins to undress while he looks on appreciatively. She climbs into bed and they start kissing. And then suddenly, out of nowhere, she pushes him away and says, "Do you think Michelle should drop piano? She just isn't enjoying it and it's costing us twenty dollars a week in lessons, and a whole Tuesday night. We could take that money and go to a movie as a family and spend quality time together instead!"

What just happened? Did she decide she really didn't want to have sex? Chances are her husband was pretty ticked, because he thought the evening was going in a certain direction, and now she's erected a big "Detour" sign.

I used to think, when I launched into a big monologue right in the middle of foreplay, that I was subconsciously trying to push my husband away. Over the years, I've realized that the opposite is the case. I can't really get into making love if I have a lot of unprocessed thoughts in my head, because they end up bouncing around in there, like a huge pinball game. My body doesn't suddenly spring into action the way my husband's does. I have to get myself in the mood, anticipate what we're doing, and concentrate if it's going to feel good. Like most women, sex for me is mostly in my head.

If there's too much other stuff rolling around in my head, my body won't be able to get in the game. Part of the process for women to get ready for the big event, then, is to empty their heads of all the stuff that's rattling around. When she can get that out, she can let other stuff in.

There's another element to this urge to talk. As we've already mentioned, men make love to feel loved, while women need to feel loved to make love. For men, making love is a way of checking in on the relationship, and making sure everything is good. When they make love with their wives, they feel as if their wives accept them and want to be with them.

Women, though, need to feel acceptance first, and part of that is feeling as if their men understand their hearts. That's why conversation is key to a woman's libido. She needs to feel as if she's understood, but she also needs to feel as if all the details in her head are out in the open so that she isn't distracted.

So if you want sex to be great, *talk*. Talk earlier in the evening so that she feels loved, and also so that she has a chance to process all the things in her head. And women, if you have a lot of logistic-type worries, discuss these with your husband; he may be able to figure out strategies to dealing with them.

Guys, understand that your wife's urge to talk isn't a rejection of you or a rejection of sex; it's her way of getting her mind in gear so that she can actually concentrate and enjoy sex.

Great Sex Challenge—Day Thirteen

Strategize with each other about developing new habits of talking earlier in the evening and checking in with each other about the day. Can you go for a walk after dinner? Can you curl up on the couch for fifteen minutes? Even keep a dayplanner near the bed so together you can go over her schedule and fit errands in it so that she's not worried. It takes twenty-one days for a habit to become ingrained, but start this one today: find regular, scheduled time just to *talk*.

This may not sound sexy, but before we can move on to how to really enjoy sex, she absolutely must be able to get her head in the game, and that means dealing with the day's stresses. Make this a habit. It will benefit both of you!

Day Fourteen: Jump In!

In movies, couples are usually totally hot for each other, so they fall into bed together. They're both "in the mood." They're both aroused. And so they make love.

That seems honest. They make love because they want to make love.

But is it true? Most women just aren't "in the mood" at the drop of a hat, panting and waiting to fall into bed. A *Psychology Today* article explained this well:

> That's what University of British Columbia psychiatrist Rosemary Basson, M.D., discovered in interviews with hundreds of women. Contrary to the conventional model, for many women, desire is not the *cause* of lovemaking, but rather, its *result*. "Women," Basson explains, "often begin sexual experiences feeling sexually neutral." But as things heat up, so do they, and they eventually experience desire.[2]

Women need to rethink what being "in the mood" actually means. Men were designed to need very little stimulation. They see

2 Michael Castleman, "Desire in Women: Does it Lead to Sex? Or Result from It?" *Psychology Today*, July 15, 2009 (http://www.psychologytoday.com/blog/all-about-sex/200907/desire-in-women-does-it-lead-sex-or-result-it).

something and they're ready to go. Women, on the other hand, need to relax, be able to concentrate on what's going on, and slowly heat up. Some men react more like women; they don't feel the urge for sex in the same way, either.

But feeling the urge first, whether you're male or female, isn't a necessary ingredient for making love. Instead, if you just jump in and embrace the thought of showing love and having fun with your spouse, chances are your body will follow.

To make love when you aren't currently "in the mood" isn't lying or being dishonest. It's just responding to your spouse. He pursues you, tries to arouse you, and then you respond. That makes perfect sense. Men, after all, tend to be the pursuer, and women tend to be the responder. That's the way we were made. Our bodies are made to respond to theirs; they weren't made to necessarily be ready before the pursuit is actually begun.

If you're the male and you're the lower-desire spouse, this is even more important. Your wife needs to feel pursued; if you wait until you feel the need for sex, even if you don't feel it very often, she's going to feel as if something is desperately missing from your relationship. You owe her more than that.

Many women are missing out on how great sex can be, and what a great sex life they can have, because they think they can't make love on account of not being "in the mood," for it would be somehow akin to faking. But to start to kiss him when he wants to make love, and to start to let your hands wander, and to respond to his hands wandering, is not faking. *It's responding*. When you put your head in the game, as Rosemary Basson found, women do tend to heat up.

Now, if you never heat up, you could have low testosterone, and if you never have sexy dreams, never get aroused, and never seem to desire sex, you should be checked for this. Alternatively, he might not have learned how to properly stimulate you, or may you don't know yourself. We'll look more at that later in the week. In general, though, if your husband has learned what your body likes, and you make a decision to respond, your body will indeed follow.

This decision is so important. If you don't make that mental leap—if you don't say, "I'm going to throw myself into this and enjoy it"—you likely won't. You have to turn on your own switch. No matter what he does, he can't arouse you unless you decide to become aroused, because we control our own sex drives.

This, too, makes sense. If women could automatically become aroused no matter who they're with, the pursuit really wouldn't be as big a deal, would it? But women don't automatically become aroused; we have to choose to let ourselves, which means we choose to enjoy our husbands. He pursues, and we choose to be caught.

Incidentally, this is what men often wish women understood. They desire sex not just for physical release, or even primarily for physical release. Sex is their way of seeing if we actually will respond to them and accept them. It's their way of seeing whether we choose them. What really interests a man is not his orgasm nearly as much as it is his wife's ability—or choice—to respond sexually.

So, how do you actually heat up? This is going to sound strange, but trust me on this: when you're making love and he's touching you, keep asking yourself, over and over, "Where do I want him to touch now? What feels good?" If you ask "Where do I want him to touch now?" then you're paying attention to your body and thinking about what it's feeling. That, in and of itself, is the key to arousal. You're not letting yourself become distracted; you're thinking about your physical body. As you do, you'll likely find that some body part does want to be touched. Just move his hand there and show him!

Guys, if you're the lower libido spouse, when you decide to initiate and focus on sex, and invite her touch, chances are your body will respond, too. Give yourself time to heat up and spend a lot of time touching, paying attention to your body's cues. Don't forsake sex, though, just because you don't have the same urge you felt when you were sixteen. She needs to feel like she's desirable, so jump in!

Great Sex Challenge—Day Fourteen

If you're the lower-desire spouse, jump in and initiate sex, even if you don't think you're in the mood. Make a decision to have a fun time and throw yourself into it. Decide to enjoy it. If you pay attention to what your body is feeling and what your body wants, your body will likely respond!

Day Fifteen: Putting the "Play" in Foreplay!

Yesterday we talked about how most women don't necessarily feel "in the mood" before they start making love; it's more a byproduct of making love. But what if you're a woman and you never actually get aroused? That's a problem.

It's likely because you're not doing enough of the things that arouse you. So today, let's talk about foreplay—what it is, how to make it great, and how to figure out what you like.

Before we do that, let's go over some misconceptions about foreplay.

1. Foreplay can get too clinical. If there's too much "spend two minutes touching her breasts and then four minutes between her legs" while she lies there, it's hardly going to be fun. It can seem like it's rote, like he's doing it just to get going, sort of like how one primes an engine before it actually turns on. If he aims for an especially sensitive area before you've spent any time kissing or holding each other, it can seem very intrusive.

For foreplay to be pleasurable, it needs to be part of the whole experience, not just something you have to do and want to get over with so you can get to the main event.

Touching and exploring each other's bodies should be fun. Foreplay, then, doesn't always have to involve the same actions for the same amount of time. If you spend a lot of time in foreplay, it can seem much more intimate, and it can make actual intercourse that much more intense.

2. Foreplay can be too much of a one-way street. If foreplay consists entirely of him touching her (because he's already in the mood, and she's not), then it can make a lot of women feel somehow inferior. What's wrong with me that I'm not ready?

Instead, make it about both of you. Women, touch him, too, so that it's about feeling each other and experiencing each other, not just him making her try to catch up to where he's already at.

3. Foreplay can become routine. While there are certain things that feel good to women, doing too much of the same thing can get boring. What really arouses a person is a whole combination of things—feeling loved, feeling a little bit teased, having all the nerves firing. You can do that in different ways. One of the sexiest things sometimes is to have him touch everything, very slowly, *except* her real erogenous zones. That makes those zones ever so much more sensitive.

You don't always have to do the same thing every night. And you don't always have to use just fingers, either. Kiss each other. Feel with the whole hand. Rub your hair over him. Be creative. The more you get involved, the more exciting and fun it will be.

4. Foreplay can be too rough. Men like to be touched intimately much more firmly than women do. Men like to be squeezed, but if a guy touches a woman's erogenous zones the way he likes to be touched, it's going to hurt—or at least be very uncomfortable. Many women, when they're new to sex, experience this and think, "I guess I don't like my breasts touched" or "I guess I don't like foreplay." That's not true Perhaps he just never touched them the way she needs to be touched!

How to Make Foreplay Wonderful

1. Tell him what you like. Women, you're going to have to communicate. If you've been married for quite some time and you've never told him that something he does turns you off, it can be even harder, because will you hurt his feelings?

I know this is a sensitive subject, but you must let him know. He likely would love to give you pleasure, but he can't know how you feel unless you tell him. If he's doing something a little bit too roughly, or not hitting exactly the right place, move his hand and show him. If you're a little brave, you can even touch yourself and show him what you like.

Sometimes showing him how to touch you is easier if you begin by asking him how he likes to be touched. Experiment a bit and say, "Harder? Softer? More? Less?" If you're asking the questions, he may return the favor.

But please tell him! Do it sensitively and you won't wreck his ego.

2. Women, be active participants. Feel him. Touch him. Change positions. Don't just lie there, waiting for him to turn you on. If you're active, the experience is more intense, and you'll enjoy it more.

3. Drag it out to relax you. Start with a bath or a massage to help you relax. Enjoy being naked together.

4. Don't rush it. Give her the proper time to get aroused, and for many women that takes a good fifteen to twenty minutes. If you're each doing things, you'll be relaxed and you'll be laughing together, and that's great. Otherwise you may feel, "After he's been touching me for two minutes I should be ready to go, so I guess we'll just start" or "I've been touching her for a few minutes so that ought to do it."

Ladies, if you're not sure what you like, and you've always been nervous about having all the attention on you during foreplay, I'd challenge you to redo the challenge from Day Five and let him touch your body for fifteen minutes while you don't move. In fact, this is a great assignment to do over and over again! It takes the pressure off you feeling like you should be ready, and it teaches him to figure out what you like (while also showing *you* what you like).

Remember, foreplay isn't optional. Most women aren't "wet" enough to make love comfortably without some stimulation first. It's not like intercourse is the main event and everything else is suboptimal. The whole experience is part of sex, not just intercourse. Foreplay is vitally important, because it helps turn the focus not just on the genitals, but on the hands, the eyes, the mouth, everything. In many ways, it's actually more personal, even more intimate, than intercourse. So try to ramp up foreplay, and you'll find sex more exciting!

Great Sex Challenge—Day Fifteen

Spend at least fifteen minutes in foreplay. Seriously. Set the timer and don't let yourself start intercourse until you've been kissing and exploring for at least fifteen minutes. Throw yourself into it, touch each other, and have fun! Your bodies are yours to explore. Don't shortchange the time!

Day Sixteen: Turning Foreplay Up a Notch

Yesterday was Foreplay Day, but it's such an important subject that it deserves another go around! Here's an email I received from a reader after my initial foreplay challenge:

> My husband really doesn't *get* foreplay. He thinks foreplay is "just for me," while sex is for "both of us," so if I want foreplay I'm being selfish, and I should do what's best for "both of us." He doesn't understand that I can't really enjoy intercourse if I don't warm up first.

That's extremely common. But part of the reason we often rush foreplay is that it seems awkward. She's lying there and he's just touching her, and everybody feels like they're watching the clock, secretly saying, "Why is this taking so long?" The woman feels as if she's being judged if she doesn't get aroused (though it's hard to get aroused when you feel rushed) and the man feels like this is really stupid because we should be getting to the main event.

We looked yesterday at some ways to make foreplay work better for her. But here are some ways to make him excited about it, too, so that both of you can embrace it as a vital part of making love!

1. Let him watch. Men are highly visual, and foreplay can begin with the way that women beckon him upstairs, or undress, or crawl into bed. Push him onto the bed and then make him watch as you take off your clothes. I know some women are very sensitive to how their bodies look, but remember that he gets pleasure from it, and your body is the only naked woman's body he's allowed to see. Let him see it!

Besides, what's sexy is often not just how your body looks but what you do with it. Tease him by taking off your underclothes slowly—or even while you're leaning over him. Run your hands over your body before you let him touch you. That's the kind of thing that will get him going!

One other thought: often the reason women like to get into their flannel pajamas, rush under the covers, and *then* get undressed is because the bedroom is *so cold*, especially in winter. That's certainly the case in Canada, where I'm from! It's good budgeting to keep the heat in the house down at night. Absolutely. But guys, if you want to turn the heat up in the bedroom, you might want to actually *turn the heat up*.

Here's a simple way to do it that will still help your bottom line: buy a space heater and put it on her side of the bed. Yes, electric heaters are very costly to run, but compared to heating a whole house, they're nothing. If you only need to have it on for fifteen or twenty minutes while you make love, it's worth it!

2. Touch him, too. Foreplay doesn't have to just be for her; it can and should also involve her touching him. And touch him everywhere, not *just* his genitals. Tease him a bit. Then ask him to show you just how he likes to be touched or stroked. Men tend to like things with a firmer hand than women do, which is why women are often too soft when they touch guys. Just ask him to guide your hand.

Now, touching him the whole time that he's stimulating her may not be the best idea, since he may not do a thorough job if he's distracted. But doing it a little bit shows that you care about his pleasure, too. It can also be highly arousing! Touch him and realize the power you have over him. He wants you. Revel in that.

3. Women, don't stay still. One reason we often feel like we should rush during foreplay is because she's just lying there, making the whole thing seem a little boring. But there's no reason you both have to lie that way. In fact, there's no reason you have to be in any *one* position for extended periods of time during foreplay. He could sit up, for instance, and then she could sit against him, so you're both facing the same direction. In that position, he can still reach around and stimulate various parts of her body, but it psychologically feels different. Many women find this a little more comfortable, because he isn't looking directly at her face.

4. Rub his body. He'll enjoy this one. If you need to be stimulated a certain way, stimulate yourself, but not with your hand. Use his body instead. Find a way to grind against his leg, or even against his penis without him entering you. This requires a lot of movement on the woman's part, which is what he'll really enjoy. It'll make it seem as if you are eager for his body, as if you're really enjoying it, which will excite him. If you keep changing positions to get an even better angle, he's going to get stimulated.

You can add some tension to it by grabbing his hands and forcing him onto his back where he has to stay, and then say something like, "Now, I'm going to use you." I guarantee there are few guys who wouldn't appreciate that. Then find ways that work, and forbid him from moving. He'll feel the sexual tension build, right as you're really enjoying yourself.

5. Kiss. Don't forget to kiss! If you're kissing, it won't seem as if there's a ticking clock in the background. You don't have to just kiss each other's mouth, either. Kiss anything! You can even kiss something innocuous, like his neck or her ears, but try to tease and drive each other crazy like that.

6. Talk. Tell each other what feels good—and this is especially important for women! Tell him you love him. Comment on what great muscles he has. Remind him of a great time you had last year on your anniversary. Say something sexy! If you're talking, you're showing him that you're enjoying this. You're into it. You're excited about participating. To men, that's a real turn-on.

Remember, what stimulates a man is often visual and psychological even more than physical. If she lets him watch her, he'll be excited. If he feels as if she's excited, having a good time, and working hard to make this wonderful, he'll be excited, too. Foreplay doesn't have to be just about getting her physically stimulated. It can be about getting her in the mood, but doing it in a way in which she reassures her husband that she's excited about being together. If you do all these things, sex won't seem like the main event anymore. It will all seem like it's part of the whole package!

Great Sex Challenge—Day Sixteen

Turn foreplay up a notch! Choose at least three of these activities and do them during foreplay tonight. I'd recommend the one about rubbing against him to stimulate her. She'll get exactly what she needs, but he'll really enjoy all the action!

Day Seventeen: Helping Her Reach the Big "O"

Last year, after my husband and I gave the "sex talk" at a FamilyLife marriage conference, I was approached by a very determined woman.

"I have a question, and I've never found anyone I could ask," she said. "What is an orgasm? And how do I know if I've had one?"

Many women don't experience orgasm during sex. In the surveys I took for *The Good Girl's Guide to Great Sex*, around sixty-five percent regularly orgasm during intercourse, but that leaves thirty-five percent who don't. Some of those thirty-five percent have never had an orgasm at all.

An orgasm is the height of sexual pleasure. While a man's orgasm is rather obvious, a woman's is not as dramatic—though it feels even better, according to some researchers. Women tend to climax right after an exquisite tension when, if your husband stopped doing whatever he was doing, you'd likely burst into tears. When women orgasm, waves pass over them. Their legs tend to stiffen up. Their head goes from side to side and their vaginal muscles contract. Plus, it feels very good.

Most women find it easier to orgasm while their husbands touch them than while they have intercourse, because the stimulation is more direct (we'll talk about why this is tomorrow). But what do you do if you've never experienced an orgasm, or if they tend to be rare?

First, that's perfectly natural. Women are more likely to orgasm once they've been married for a few years, so if it takes a while for things to work, that's okay. Orgasm is the ultimate letting go. When you're still shy, early in your marriage, that can be difficult. Don't worry about it. The more you worry about it, the less likely you are to get there.

Here are some tips to making it more likely.

Relax. To orgasm, you really need to be swept away by the moment and the feeling. If something is distracting you, it's hard to be swept away. That's why it's unlikely to happen if you're tense. The best thing you can do is relax! Don't worry about it; it will happen one day once your body is used to pleasure.

Move. Don't lie there, waiting for it to come upon you. Remain an active participant as you make love. Switch positions, even if just a little bit, so that it feels good. Tilt your body. Move on top sometimes. Take his hand and move it where you'd like to be stimulated, even during intercourse. The more you take the initiative, the sexier you'll feel.

Concentrate on "feeling good." Here's the most important tip. Concentrate on "feeling good," not on reaching orgasm. Make pleasure your goal. As you're making love, concentrate on the pleasure. Ask yourself, "What feels good? Where do I want my husband to touch me now?" That'll help you zero in on anything arousing. Then slowly let it carry you away.

Breathe. Just like they say in exercise class, don't forget to breathe! Orgasm needs oxygen, and it's easier to relax if you breathe.

Often we have a hard time relaxing, so we stop breathing because we feel like we're oh-so-close. Believe me, breathing won't stop the orgasm. It will actually help you feel the pleasure more and the waves will be more likely to start. If you tense up, waiting for that orgasm, sometimes you start aiming for it too much and it becomes elusive. If you concentrate on pleasure first, and then on learning to relax, it's more likely to happen.

A note to him: If you put too much pressure on your wife to orgasm, and feel like a failure if she doesn't, she's less likely to want to make love. It's great to want to pleasure her, but pressuring her can backfire. Just take things slowly, laugh a lot, leave time to explore, and let things happen as they happen.

Now, if you're consistently reaching climax before she does, please don't leave her hanging. Make it a habit to help her afterwards, by stimulating her clitoris or anything else she finds pleasurable. If she's consistently frustrated, that will increase her tension about not being able to reach orgasm, making it more difficult to achieve this.

Great Sex Challenge—Day Seventeen

Redo yesterday's challenge to concentrate on foreplay, then take it one step further. If she's never experienced an orgasm, try to prolong foreplay to see if it happens. In fact, if you're up for it, don't give up until it happens! Some couples have tried this, even if it takes hours, and the relief is so immense. Women, concentrate on the pleasure, concentrate on what your body is feeling, and relax. If she has experienced orgasm through ways other than intercourse, but has a hard time experiencing one through intercourse, spend a ton of time on foreplay and only start making love when she's very excited. Ladies, keep concentrating on what your body is feeling, and learn to revel in the pleasure.

If orgasm is still elusive in your marriage, I have three chapters in *The Good Girl's Guide to Great Sex* on how to make sex feel great—including what to do if that orgasm just won't occur.

Day Eighteen: The Pleasure Center

"I just don't understand what the big deal is about sex." I hear that from women all the time. People may look breathless in movies, but sex sure doesn't take their breath away. When women have that kind of attitude, men feel deflated. They want to be wanted, not just placated.

Today we're going to try to show her what the big deal is! Many women simply have not experienced physically wonderful sex. After all, it's kind of tricky for us, because we're not guaranteed pleasure in the way men are. Once women experience real passion, frequency does increase. But the passion itself is what men often crave. It's not just the release; it's seeing her receive and experience pleasure.

How can we experience pleasure? We've talked about foreplay and how to relax and experience orgasm, but let's get a little more technical (which will end up meaning we'll have more fun).

Here's the thing about orgasm for women: pretty much all orgasms are caused by the clitoris (that little knob of flesh in front of the vagina) being stimulated or pressed. The vagina itself doesn't have that many nerves; the clitoris, as tiny as it is, actually has more nerves than the penis. The clitoris is a little bundle of pleasure.

But because it's little, it often doesn't get a lot of stimulation once intercourse starts. Here are a few tips for making sure your clitoris gets the attention it needs.

1. Change up the missionary position. Ladies, tilt your pelvis up when you're on the bottom. If he's on top and you just lie there, you won't actually experience a lot of stimulation. Tilt up, though, and you'll put pressure on the clitoris, changing the angle so that his pelvic bone comes in contact with you there during intercourse. So try tilting up (just by squeezing your butt muscles, so to speak). It's a little change, but it does a lot! By squeezing your muscles, you'll engage the clitoris and it will feel better in and of itself.

2. Put her on top. Make love with her on top. Then have her very slowly try to change the angle so she can hit him at the right spot that makes her feel good. Just keep rotating gradually until it feels good.

3. Touch her during intercourse. If you're trying other positions, have him put a finger or two on her clitoris, so that she receives stimulation during intercourse.

She often feels great during foreplay because he's directly stimulating her where it feels good, but the simulation stops when you start actual intercourse. That's often why women have a hard time reaching orgasm. If you make love in different positions—like rear entry, or spooning—he can put his fingers on the clitoris to provide pressure at the same time. One little tip for guys: don't concentrate on rubbing her clitoris if you do this; just put your finger there. The pressure is all she needs, and with you thrusting, you're likely to rub a little bit too roughly. It's better to just provide pressure than to try much else.

I have many more tips in *The Good Girl's Guide to Great Sex*, but here's one that hopefully will help you quickly! Many women feel as if something must be wrong with them because intercourse itself just doesn't feel that wonderful. That's actually quite normal. Because the vagina doesn't have many nerves, unless you're making an effort to have her clitoris line up with the base of his pelvis, she isn't going to get the pleasurable feelings she needs. There's nothing wrong with her. You both need to adjust your position a little bit!

I received an email from a woman lately that said this:

> I'm always hearing about all kinds of different positions, and I do want to have a fun and varied sex life! But to tell you the truth, there's really only one position that works for me. I can't orgasm any other way. What's wrong with me?

Absolutely nothing. She's very normal! Perhaps you've had to rotate and tilt to get the angle just right, and with the shape of his body, and the shape of hers, there's one position that tends to be more conducive to orgasm. And it's not the same position for each woman. If you enjoy other positions, but you find that only one lets her orgasm, that's really okay. You can always use the others as a type of foreplay, and then finish in one. It doesn't mean she's inferior if she doesn't benefit from sexual gymnastics!

Incidentally, as women try to find the right position, it also means you'll both have to be more active while you make love. You won't be able to just lie there. You'll have to shift a bit, or tilt a bit, and that means you'll be more engaged. Your husband will likely appreciate this, because it'll show that you want to make love, that you are choosing to receive pleasure. That's a big deal to a man. Even if it takes you a few tries (or a lot of tries) to get it right, he'll really enjoy your effort (and likely so will you).

Great Sex Challenge—Day Eighteen

Tonight, try a position or two, but stop him from moving. Instead, give her time to rotate to experiment with getting the angle right. This takes some courage and assertiveness. She'll have to speak up! If it doesn't feel just right, keep trying. Change positions if you have to. Just don't "settle" for something. Ladies, tell him what feels good and keep working at it until you find it!

Day Nineteen: Little Changes that Feel Amazing For Her

Sometimes the smallest changes can make the biggest impact! Yesterday we talked about tilting your pelvis; today we're going to list some things men can do to make sex feel that much better for her. Guys, here we go.

Let the tension build. Teasing and building tension often makes sex far more pleasurable for women than just jumping in, because the teasing helps her anticipate what's coming next. Since sex for women is so much in our heads, we need that chance to look forward!

When you're making love, don't thrust all the way in at the start. Start shallow and slow, growing more deliberate—and going deeper—as she starts to feel more aroused. Sometimes, of course, she'll like things more quickly, but encourage her to set the pace. If you start in before she's ready, she often will never have a chance to catch up.

Use lubrication when needed. Some women have a harder time "getting wet," and sex, when you're not well-lubricated, doesn't feel that good. If you add some lubrication, such as Astroglide or K-Y

Jelly, she'll feel more pleasure. This should never replace foreplay, but at times lubrication can be handy, such as when trying a new position, when enjoying a "quickie," or even when going through menopause, when hormones are all over the place. When she's well-lubricated, her body will respond better to intercourse.

Breast attention. Breasts are funny things. Some women enjoy their nipples being stimulated and some don't. Just because she doesn't like it during foreplay doesn't mean she won't like it later on. Often women whose nipples are very sensitive when they aren't aroused enjoy being pinched right before orgasm. So experiment a little. The best way to tell is for her to start being aware of her own body. Ladies, pay attention to your body's cues. If something will feel pleasurable, chances are it will start to give you signals. So ask yourself what wants to be touched next. You may find that your breasts do respond later, near the end of the encounter.

Locate her G-spot. Finally, we have that elusive G-spot. Yesterday I said the clitoris will trigger almost all orgasms, and that's mostly true. Many women, however, also swear by the G-spot, a small oval of knobby flesh located about one-and-a-half to three inches up the front wall of the vagina (the wall that's against her stomach, not her back). It's not right on the surface, but about one centimeter below, so it's a little difficult to stimulate. Because it's on the front wall, it's on the top when you're in the missionary position, which can make it a little more difficult to find. Some researchers believe it's simply an extension of the clitoris, and so they're one and the same thing. Others think it doesn't exist at all.

My feeling is that we should never feel dysfunctional if we can't find it, since large scale studies have failed to consistently show a definite anatomical location for it. Many women swear by it, though, and since the research is bound to be fun, why not try? It will feel good even if you don't find the G-spot.

You can attempt to locate it either by having him insert his fingers (after applying lubricant!) or through intercourse. Some people find that the spooning position, when you're lying on your sides facing the same direction, or the woman-on-top position works best. You'll know when you find it; it's often a very intense rush, with orgasm soon afterward.

Great Sex Challenge—Day Nineteen

Pick one or two new things and try them tonight. Don't limit yourself to what's written here. Guys, ask her what she thinks would make sex feel amazing, because she may have some ideas she's been afraid to share. Don't take it personally if she asks you to do something differently; just take it to mean that she's committed to improving your sex life. Ladies, open up and let him know what you want. The sky's the limit!

Day Twenty: Little Changes that Feel Amazing for Him

Guys don't usually have as much trouble feeling physical pleasure from sex as women. But that doesn't mean we can't make small changes to help him feel even more amazing!

Ladies, here are a few tips to make sex extra special for him.

Move. Too often, women can fall into the trap of thinking that what really matters to a guy is sexual release. He needs his orgasm, and then he's fine. But remember that a man's whole identity is wrapped up in his sexuality. He doesn't just need sexual release; he needs the feeling of acceptance and love he gets from knowing his wife actually wants to make love to him. She doesn't just *let* him. She *wants* him.

For a guy to feel great, then, you need to show him that you're enjoying this! So much of his pleasure is wrapped up in the idea that he can give you pleasure. So don't just lie there. Move! Run your hands over his back. Try a new position. Respond to his thrusts by moving your hips. Show that you're into it.

Vocalize. And don't just move—moan. Or talk. Or say something! Guys love hearing feedback that what they're doing feels good.

Remember his erogenous zones. Women have lots of sensitive areas. We tend to focus on more areas of a woman's body during sex than on a man's, because she needs the attention to get aroused during foreplay. In so doing, we can shortchange the guys. Contrary to common practice, they actually do have more than one erogenous zone. Many men find their nipples sensitive, or their necks or earlobes, or behind their knees. Pay attention to other parts of his body, too, especially his ears and neck, when you're making love. This will make it more intimate and intense for him.

Squeeze him. While the ego boost of showing him you're enjoying it is awesome, a few physical cues can send him to ecstasy. One of the most pleasurable things you can do is squeeze him while he's inside you, using your Kegel muscles. Those are the muscles of your pelvic floor, which can open and contract your vagina. You may not have noticed them before, but if you stop the flow of urine when you're peeing, you'll be activating the same muscles.

When you're making love, make that same movement and squeeze him. You can hold the squeeze, or, if your muscles are strong, you can squeeze rhythmically to his thrusts. To get used to the idea, have him enter you but then remain still. You can practice trying to squeeze and relax, squeeze and relax, and see if he notices the difference.

Let him go deeper. Another thing that's especially pleasurable is to find a position that lets him thrust even more deeply. This isn't something to try when you're just getting used to making love, or when you're sore. If you're ready, wrap your legs around his back, or even rest your feet on his shoulders (if you're flexible enough).

Now, guys, if she's doing this, she's making herself really vulnerable (which, of course, is part of what makes it exciting). Treat her well, and make sure she isn't uncomfortable. Go slowly at first!

Great Sex Challenge—Day Twenty

Talk together about which of these he'd like to try—and if he wants to try the more adventurous physical ones, let this challenge last two days! Guys, this is the night to let her know what it means to you that she's enjoying sex, too. Explain to her how you feel when you know that she's excited to make love. Let her know what sorts of things she can do or say to reassure you when you're making love.

If you want to try the physical challenges, take it slowly and learn together. Then show her some appreciation for stretching her limits!

Timeout Three: Feeling Alive Again

When I posted this series online, I began to receive a series of quite distressing emails at this point. For many people, sex had become such a difficult part of their lives. It had become twisted, dirty, shameful, or simply nonexistent. As I read these emails, I thought, *Why are we letting something God made to be beautiful become a negative thing in our lives? Why are we settling for that?* We mustn't let something beautiful be stolen from us anymore.

If you're not having any of these thoughts, feel free to move on to Day Twenty-One. If you're having these doubts, I understand. But I ache for you.

When the beauty of making love is stolen from you, it is so sad, so barren. One of the telltale signs that something is from God is that something is *alive*. Life is from God. Being *teeming* with life is from God. And so the opposite—death—is not from God. Think about this. When evil triumphs, it's not usually categorized by luscious trees or plants or beautiful things. It's ugly. Even if it starts out beautiful, the ugliness takes over.

When the Mongols rampaged across Asia and the Middle East in the thirteenth century, they left behind devastation—and desert. Many places that were not formerly deserts became deserts over the next few decades because the Mongols burned everything. Without plants, the land dried up. Destruction kills what is alive.

If you're not a history buff, think about *The Lord of the Rings*, and compare Mordor with the Shire. The Shire is alive; when Sauron took over Mordor, he made sure everything that was living died (except for his minions also bent on destruction).

I noticed this phenomenon in 1989 when I visited East Berlin. West Berlin was beautiful, with trees and parks and art and lovely buildings. East Berlin was Spartan. Everything was utilitarian. Joy was gone.

Evil doesn't just propagate evil, you see. It also tries to destroy that which is beautiful.

This morning, I was reading in my devotions the story of Ezekiel and the dry bones, found in Ezekiel 37. God calls on Ezekiel to prophesy over dead bones, and as he does, the bones begin to rattle. They form together. Sinews grow on them. Then flesh. But they're still dead until God breathes into them.

I think that's a picture of where many of us are today when it comes to sex. We feel dead. We're not excited about it. It doesn't grow our relationship; it eats away at it. So, what's our response?

This story shows two things. One, those bones listened to Ezekiel's prophecy and joined together and grew. Two, they weren't fully alive until God breathed into them (I know I'm taking liberties with it here, but bear with me!)

What does that mean for you?

Listen to the Truth

God wants you to be *alive*. With God, life is teeming, abundant, lush, tropical, and beautiful. Even if your sex life isn't like that, understand that this is what God wants for you.

Then agree with God. You're not agreeing because you're not experiencing it; you may very well not be experiencing much of anything. Nonetheless, agree with God that this is the way He meant it to be. Agree with your spouse, the two of you together, that this is how God wants it to be.

Let me say a word to the spouse, whether it's the husband or wife, who has the low libido: you need to believe this, too. God does not want you this way. He did not design you this way. He wants your marriage to be alive and fun and passionate. If you feel inadequate, don't shrug your shoulders and say, "Oh, well, there's nothing I can do. That's just the way I am." That's a copout.

If you are severely overweight, you don't just say, "That's just the way I am." You say, "I need to lose some weight, even if it's hard." If you're consumed by nightmares because of things done to you in the past, you don't just say, "I guess I'll never sleep again." You get help. And yet somehow, when it comes to sex, we seem content to say, "I guess this is just the way I am."

No, it's not! God wants you to be fully alive and passionate. If you're not there, at least agree with God that this is His design.

Move Together to Make it Happen

Once you've agreed, you've got to actually take steps forward. Those bones started joining together. Sinews were formed. So *do* something! That may mean going back to the beginning of this series and rereading some of the challenges. It may mean going over some of the more challenging ones and really putting your heart into it. Instead of balking, this may mean admitting, "It scares me a little. It pushes me out of my comfort zone. But I know God wants me to experience passion, so I'm going to try.

Let God In

Here's the final one, and really the most important: you can agree with God all you want. You can try to get things going in the right direction, but ultimately you cannot do this by yourself. You can't *will* yourself to be passionate.

It is God who breathed life into those dry bones.

All of us need a breath from God today, even those of us who don't feel particularly bad about our sex lives. All of us need more passion. When we let God in and feel closer to Him, letting Him work, we feel so much more alive, both spiritually and sexually. When we feel dry spiritually, we often feel dry sexually.

The opposite is also true. If you want to be fully alive and fully passionate, you need to be passionate about God first, and let Him move. That will have major ripple effects in the bedroom.

Timeout Challenge

Pray as a couple. Take each other's hands and earnestly pray together for your sex and spiritual life. Pray that God will breathe passion into you—passion that will be felt both inside and outside the bedroom. Pray that you will know what it is to feel fully alive in Him. Don't just pray quick prayers. Wrestle in prayer before God.

Maybe you have a hard time praying as a couple. That's okay, but try to pray for at least a few minutes. Pray about your kids. Pray about your friends. As you come together spiritually, you will feel your spirits grow more connected. As you ask God together for Him to bless your sex life; that prayer will be powerful. So, pray and see God work.

If you're not comfortable praying, or you just aren't religious, you can journal together, talk together, or take a walk in nature together. Even write a mission statement of what you want your marriage to be. But if you can pray, please do so. The God who created sex is also the One who can make it stupendous!

Days 21–25:

True Oneness in the Bedroom (Spiritual Intimacy)

Day Twenty-One: Experiencing Spiritual Oneness when You Make Love

In many ways, today's post is the most important of this series. Sex is supposed to be a truly spiritual union. Let me explain.

If you grew up in the church, chances are you grew up with the King James Bible. Do you remember hearing Genesis read out loud?

> And Adam knew Eve his wife; and she conceived, and bare [a son], and said, I have gotten a man from the Lord. (Genesis 4:1, KJV)

We'd sit there and giggle and elbow our friends, because we thought it was so funny. Instead of saying a word that meant "sex", the Bible said "knew." Because obviously God was embarrassed.

Hold on a second. What if there was something else going on?

You see, in Psalm 139:23, David says, *"Search me, O God, and know my heart."* In fact, that theme (begging God to dig deep inside our hearts and really *know* us) is used throughout Scripture. The same Hebrew word here used for "know" is used to represent our deep longing for a union with God and the sexual union between a husband and a wife.

What if there's a connection? What if sex isn't just supposed to be a physical union? Perhaps it's also supposed to encompass this deep longing to be known, the way that David yearned for God.

I think that's part of God's plan for sex. Think about it. In sex, we bare ourselves physically. But for sex to work well, we also have to bare ourselves emotionally. We have to be able to be vulnerable. We have to be willing to "let go." Women have to let men in, emotionally, to even get aroused. Men have to let their guard down, too, in order to experience the kind of love they long for.

God created people with a desperate longing for relationship. We long to know and be known, and in that knowing be accepted. It's our deepest need. God gave us this drive to know Him and be known by Him, but He also gave us these sexual longings to be truly and wonderfully *known*.

I talk about this at great length in *The Good Girl's Guide to Great Sex*, and look at how we can make this spiritual longing and spiritual intimacy part of the sexual experience. I truly believe that it's the spiritual intimacy that people actually crave most.

When we focus only on the physical, sex too often can seem shallow. When we combine the physical with the emotional and spiritual, sex is stupendous, because it encompasses all that we are. One of the reasons our culture has become more pornographic—and why things that were once considered sexually taboo are now mainstream—is that our culture has made sex into something only physical, because they don't have anything else. They know they're missing something, so they try more and more extreme things.

We who are married have the real deal. We have the ingredients for an amazing sexual relationship, because it's real intimacy, not just orgasm—and intimacy, in fact, makes orgasm even greater! The women who were most likely to orgasm in the surveys I took were Christian women. When you're in a lifetime-committed relationship, you're more likely to experience all the great aspects of sex, not just the physical.

The spiritual union that is part of sex isn't something out of the Kama Sutra or some eastern thing. That's not what I'm talking about.

I'm talking about our deep hunger to connect. To me, that's actually more profound, and more of an aphrodisiac, than the thought of something specifically physical.

But how can we experience spiritual intimacy while making love? Here are some practical thoughts.

1. Take time being naked. I don't just mean taking your clothes off to make love. I mean actually being naked together. Hold each other. Take a bath together. Even pray naked together! Redo that exercise where you just take time touching each other's bodies. Feel as if you completely know the other person. It's actually more vulnerable to be naked while someone touches you than just to be naked while you have sex. So take that time to explore!

2. Take time to be spiritually naked. This may sound weird, but trust me on it: pray before sex. Or at least read a Psalm or something. When we unite spiritually, it's as if our souls are drawn together. When our souls are drawn together, we want to draw together in a deeper way. So keep a Bible by the bed and just read passages at nighttime. Try to pray together. If you're uncomfortable with freeform prayer, buy a book of prayers, or use the Anglican prayer book. The words don't matter; the heart does. When you mean it, and you bow before God together, you really are drawn towards each other in a more intense way.

3. Look into each other's eyes. The eyes are windows, yet how often do we close our eyes, as if we're trying to shut the other person out, and concentrate on ourselves? I know sometimes you have to close your eyes to feel everything, but occasionally open up and look into each other's eyes. Actually seeing your spouse—and letting your spouse see into you—is very intimate, especially at the height of passion.

4. Say "I love you." It's such a little thing, but while you're making love, or even when you orgasm, say "I love you." Make sex about not just feeling good, but expressing love. Say your spouse's name. Show him or her that you're completely captivated.

5. Desire your spouse. Spiritual intimacy during sex ultimately depends on your desire to be united with your spouse. That desire is fed throughout the day by concentrating on what you love about each other, by thinking about each other, by flirting and playing together, by saying positive things about each other to friends. It isn't something that "just happens." It's the culmination of a relationship you already have.

I truly believe that for many couples this is *the* major roadblock to sex being everything it can be. Tomorrow we'll be dissecting some of the problems with spiritual intimacy and sex a little more, but I think many people have bought into this idea that sex is only physical, when really sex is the physical expression of a deep drive we have to be connected to one another.

I recently received a comment from a woman who said this:

> I always thought, "Oh sex is just something that *he* needs. I can do fine without it." So not true. I need it too! We have connected in amazing ways, in and out of the bedroom, and I am so excited to have my old husband back!

For the women who are reading this, sex *isn't* something he needs just for physical release; he needs it to feel really intimate. And we need that, too! Many of us push sex out of the way because it seems like a chore, but what we're really doing is denying ourselves one of the most powerful tools we have to feel truly connected and accepted by another individual.

If sex makes you feel dirty, or is a constant source of conflict, then wait until tomorrow's challenge. But if it's simply that you've never experienced sex this way, try those steps. Concentrate on what you love about each other. Pray together. Memorize each other's bodies. Say "I love you." Look into each other's eyes. Truly be joined. There really is nothing else like it.

Great Sex Challenge—Day Twenty-One

Make love, don't just have sex. Tonight, while you're together, do your best to show your spouse how much you love him or her. While you're making love, concentrate on all the things you love about him or her. Be passionate about it! See what happens.

Day Twenty-Two: Being Mentally Present While You Make Love

Feeling totally one with your spouse is a beautiful thing. It's intense, and that intensity often makes the physical side even better.

Just because sex physically feels good, though, doesn't mean it's going to feel like we're one, and that's because many people, when they make love, aren't mentally present. They're thinking of something else, and so their bodies respond to fantasy, not reality. It isn't your spouse who captures your attention; it's an image from a movie, or a book, or pornography, or even a memory. That will wreck your chances of experiencing intimacy.

Unfortunately, though, sex in our pornographic culture has often been reduced to the physical. What's arousing isn't a person but an image. We therefore find it very difficult to get aroused during sex without first concentrating on an image. In fact, psychologists have even coined a new term for those who can't maintain an erection, or who can't stay aroused with their spouse: Sexual Attention Deficit Disorder. These people require additional stimulus, like porn or erotica.

My husband's a physician, and when he was in medical school, he was taught that when you're counseling a couple with sexual problems, you should recommend they watch porn together. Porn has become mainstream. Yet it isn't harmless. The more our bodies become aroused by an external stimulus, like pornography, the more our bodies start to require that stimulus in order to become aroused. The feeling—arousal—is now associated primarily with that stimulus. Just being with your spouse and touching your spouse isn't enough anymore.

To compound the problem, when people use pornography (and it's not just men; thirty percent of porn users are female), they usually masturbate as well. They spend their sexual energy on pornography rather than on their marriage. That diminishes their desire for their spouse and is one of the leading causes of lack of libido. When you get your satisfaction elsewhere, your spouse isn't enough anymore. That's going to hurt your spouse. Women, especially, feel ugly and unwanted. Even if guys who use porn swear it has nothing to do with their wives, and they still love their wives, women will rightly interpret this as a form of cheating. When you get aroused by an image of someone else, and then masturbate to that image, it's virtually the same as cheating.

While many women also use porn, our weakness tends to be erotica. Novels like *50 Shades of Grey* sell like hotcakes to sexually frustrated moms, and people think of it as harmless. It simply gets her in the mood! That's a good thing, right?

Nope. While she may be in the mood, she's in the mood because of a fantasy, not because of her husband. When she makes love, it's the fantasy that turns her on, not her husband. The more we use something else to get aroused, the less our spouse is able to arouse us, and the more difficulty we have staying "mentally present" while making love.

What does being mentally present look like?

We Won't Focus on Something Else

We'll make the decision not to think about a pornographic image or a storyline or past lover. We'll concentrate on how much we love our spouse and on how exciting our spouse is. That will be virtually impossible to do if we're still filling our mind with porn or erotica. You must give that up. Just like an alcoholic has to say no to alcohol, say no to what's stealing your sexual energy.

For many people, that means accountability. Get controls on your computer. Share your account on your e-reader so that your spouse can see what you're reading. Get a same-sex accountability partner you can have coffee with who will challenge you to remain faithful in every way—and you do the same for him or her.

We'll Think Sexy Thoughts about our Spouse

Personally, I don't think there's anything wrong with remembering something wonderful you did together that was stupendous, or imaging being on a beach, or whatever it may be for you. But fantasizing about someone who isn't your spouse, or bringing up pornographic images to get aroused, isn't right. It hinders your ability to really bond with your spouse.

We'll Give Ourselves Grace

Remaining mentally present is tricky when we have a history of porn. If either of you shortcuts the arousal cycle by pulling up pornographic images, ask God to help you stop, and then practice just being present. Think about your body. Think about your spouse. Trace your fingers along your spouse's body. Think specifically about what feels good and what you love about your spouse, and then say some of these things out loud. Keep your mind focused on the here and now and you'll find it a much more intimate, and intense, experience.

If you do find that images start to interfere, stop what you're doing for a minute and just talk and kiss again, until you find that your mind is back where it should be.

If your spouse is the one dealing with this, extend grace. It hurts to know that your spouse struggles with fantasy, but it's so much better to give him or her a safe place to admit when they're struggling than it is to humiliate them and make them afraid to tell you. If you want honesty and intimacy in the bedroom, you have to give your spouse room to admit when they're having problems—and you have to dedicate yourself to helping them get over it. Remember, the point is the direction you're moving in, not the place you've come from. Don't get mad at the past. Join together to head towards a better sex life in the future.

Great Sex Challenge—Day Twenty-Two

Make love, but if you feel your mind wandering, stop and talk to your spouse. Think to yourself, "What feels good? What do I want him or her to do now?" Concentrate on your spouse's body and on what your own body is experiencing. Tell your spouse if you need to stop and start over. Practice being mentally present. It makes sex so much more intense!

Day Twenty-Three: Trying New Positions

It may seem strange to talk about positions in the section on spiritual intimacy, but for the next few days I want to explore how we decide what's okay to do, and how we can add more fun to the bedroom without compromising intimacy.

One of the problems many couples have is that they see sex almost solely in physical terms. It's not about bringing you close as much as it is about bringing you pleasure.

I think it should be both. Yet when many couples discuss their sexual boundaries, they enter a landmine. If you forget that sex is supposed to be an intimate thing, and not only an orgasmic thing, you can go astray and actually cheapen sex.

I placed these challenges within the spiritual intimacy section to remind us that when we try new things, it should be to increase the fun quotient and to feel closer, not to humiliate anyone or to act selfishly.

So let's talk today about positions. I've heard it said that the man-on-top, woman-on-bottom position is called the missionary position, because missionaries taught that it was the only "proper" position. That's really a myth that makes missionaries sound uptight!

Is there really a "holy" position? And if we're talking about experiencing spiritual intimacy, not just physical intimacy, are some positions wrong while others are right?

I'm only referring to vaginal intercourse positions here, but I truly believe that when it comes to vaginal intercourse, any way that two married adults choose to connect is perfectly fine. You're just joining your bodies, and it's not like only one position is ordained by God. In fact, it's never even mentioned in the Bible.

The missionary position is often thought to be holier because it allows the couple to kiss and look into each other's eyes at the same time. But so does the woman-on-top position, or the making-love-while-sitting (or even standing) position. So that argument doesn't really hold water.

I think the reason that missionary is considered holy is because sex is often thought of as shameful (especially for women). Any position that involves a woman being active is thought of as a little bit wrong (or even a lot wrong). It's somehow unseemly. A man can thrust, because males are supposed to feel sexual pleasure, but for a woman to want to move—well, that may mean she's enjoying herself too much.

That doesn't mean I'm against missionary—not at all! For many women, it's actually quite pleasurable, especially if they're able to achieve the right angle by tilting their pelvis. And it is very romantic.

Nevertheless, it has some drawbacks. It's difficult if there's a big weight discrepancy between the two of you, or if she's pregnant. If she's nervous, feeling in control by being on top often relieves stress. And stimulating the G-spot is easier using other positions.

Often a couple will find that one or two positions tend to be their favorites, because it's easier for her to reach orgasm using them. Yet trying and using new positions has benefits other than orgasm. It makes sex more active and less routine. It requires a bit of extra effort, which tells your spouse, "I'm excited about doing this tonight." It can even increase intimacy because you say to your spouse, "I really want to explore you and know everything I can about how you work." This brings a new level of vulnerability, which can increase our feelings of closeness.

One couple I know uses the "Rule of 3" when making love—they can't make love more than three times in a row in the same position.

They switch it up, so that it doesn't get boring. If you find it easier to orgasm in one particular position, that's okay. Just use the other positions as foreplay.

Here are the six most typical positions to try. Every other position is really a variant of one of these.

1. Man on top. The missionary position. You lie together, him on top, nose to nose, breast to breast.

Make it feel great: Tilt her hips up. Use a pillow if you want, but the important thing is to engage her muscles to apply pressure to the clitoris, not just to raise her hips.

Variations: She can put her legs on his back (or, if she's flexible, on his shoulders. This allows deeper penetration).

2. Woman on top. He lies down in bed, and she climbs on top of him in a sitting position.

Make it Feel Great: Let her determine the depth of thrusting and let her vary the angle until she gets the most contact with her clitoris. This position is best for women who are nervous.

Variations: She can lie down against him, similar to missionary position but with her on top. The thrusting will then take more energy (and likely burn more calories). She can also vary how she sits. If she sits instead of kneels, she'll get deeper penetration, too. For the really adventurous, she can turn around so she's facing his feet, leaning backwards against him. That way, he can easily touch her breasts and clitoris while she does the thrusting.

3. Sitting position. He sits, either against the bed or in a chair, and she straddles him.

Make it feel great: Lean backwards to change the angle a bit. Find an angle that works best for stimulating her.

Variations: Don't lean against anything, but lock your legs around each other for stability. This one's a little more challenging, but the extra effort can be intense.

4. Woman lying down, man standing up. She lies down, with her legs hanging off of the bed. He stands between her legs. This allows for deeper penetration as well.

Make it feel great: Use lubrication! In this position, he can thrust much more deeply than usual, so make sure it's comfortable for her.

Variations: She lies down, he kneels on the bed between her legs.

5. Standing against a wall. She leans herself against a wall and wraps her legs around his torso for support. He stands facing her. This requires a lot of balance and strength, which often detracts from the pleasure.

Make it feel great: This is more of a fun, rip-your-clothes-off-I-can't-wait-another-minute position rather than it is a position for the whole encounter. It's fun sometimes to start out this way, but you'll likely want to head over to the bed or a chair or you'll run out of steam.

Variations: She's on the kitchen counter or dresser, and he's standing. This is similar, although again, this is more a position for a breathless encounter than it is a drawn out one that feels pleasurable for her.

6. Rear entry. She kneels on all fours on the bed. He kneels behind her, facing the same direction. This position is the most difficult to get right, because sometimes you have to play around with the angle in order to achieve penetration. This isn't a position to try early on your honeymoon if you're a virgin on your wedding day. Get comfortable fitting together first. However, once you do fit together, some couples swear that this feels the most pleasurable.

Make it feel great: he can reach around and put a finger or two on her clitoris to increase her stimulation. She can also vary the angle of her body so that the penis hits her at different angles. Some women find this is the best way to find the G-spot. How do you know when you find it? He'll be thrusting, and you'll suddenly feel like you're about to orgasm, even if you hadn't been that aroused yet.

Variations: Lie in bed on your sides, facing the same direction, with him behind. This one is often the easiest during the latter stages of pregnancy.

Great Sex Challenge—Day Twenty-Two

Pick at least three positions and try all of them tonight! Start with one and then move on to the others. Afterwards, talk about it. Would you like to implement something like the "Rule of 3," where you use different positions? Is there a position you like best or find most pleasurable? Share that with your spouse.

Day Twenty-Four: Deciding Your Sexual Boundaries

In any marriage, one spouse is going to feel more adventurous in the bedroom than the other.

Last week, we concentrated primarily on how to create fireworks. This week, we have turned to how to experience spiritual intimacy, and complete oneness, when we make love. It's good for both of those subjects to be present as context for what we're going to talk about today.

How do you decide what's okay to do and what's not?

Over the last few years, the vast majority of anonymous questions I've received have been about this—"My husband (or wife) wants to try something in bed, and I'm not comfortable with it. What do I do?"

Let's look at some basic ground rules to guide us.

1. Our whole body is for sex. Sex is supposed to be fun. God made our bodies to feel great during sex—and He didn't create it so that only certain body parts feel good. As we mentioned in our discussion about foreplay, the more you involve other body parts, the better! When you read Song of Solomon, you'll find tributes to just about everything. Sometimes, however, we get hung up and think that only certain positions are holy, and everything else is somehow wrong.

I don't buy that. We're supposed to get lost in each other, to enjoy all of each other. That's part of the celebration of being intimate and naked together.

2. Sex is more than physical. At the same time, sex is more than just a physical connection. It's also a spiritual and emotional connection. One of the reasons, I believe, that married Christians tend to enjoy sex more than those who aren't married is that we know it isn't just about the physical. When we make love, we're also expressing our commitment for one another and our hunger for true intimacy.

The world doesn't understand this concept because our culture has divorced sex from relationship and commitment. All they have is the physical. That's why our culture has become increasingly pornographic. When the physical is all you have, eventually the physical feels empty. To get the same high, you have to do more and more extreme things (in the same way that an alcoholic needs to take more drinks to get the same buzz). That's why things that were once taboo are now talked about openly on sitcoms.

Our pornographic culture will inevitably impact our own idea of sexuality. If what is portrayed as sexy are these extreme things—threesomes, sex toys, etc.—then some of us will get very enticed by that.

My caution is this: while there is freedom in the marriage bed, and while the whole body is good, if you start seeing sex in terms of riskier and more perverse things, you may lessen its ability to truly bring you and your spouse together intimately. You may lose the spiritual connection.

Be careful that you always experience sex, first and foremost, as a way to say "I love you," and not just as a way to get selfish fantasies met.

3. There is great freedom. Nevertheless, there is great freedom in the marriage bed, and I'd be hesitant to pronounce anything sinful that doesn't involve a third party—or involve fantasizing specifically about a third party (like pornography). That being said, just because something isn't sinful doesn't mean it's good to do. Like 1 Corinthians 6:12 says, *"'All things are lawful [permissible] for me,' but not all things are helpful."*

4. While acts may not be sinful, selfishness is. I have one more caveat, and I'll use oral sex as an example. I don't believe this is sinful, and I believe it can be argued that Song of Solomon alludes to it. Kissing is fine, and the mouth has more germs than most other parts of the body, so if you'll kiss a mouth, I don't think there's a big problem with kissing other parts of the body—if you're comfortable with that.

However, I received an email from a woman recently who said that her husband demands that they start every encounter this way—and often do this in place of intercourse. There were other issues as well, but the simple fact was that he preferred this to kissing her mouth or even to any shared physical pleasure, like intercourse. That's just pure and simple selfishness.

There's nothing wrong with being "giving" during a particular sexual encounter and concentrating on one of you for a time, but if that becomes the majority of your sex life together, there's a huge problem. That's not real intimacy; that's just being selfish. *And it needs to stop.*

Let me say something specifically to those of you who are the more adventurous spouse. It's also selfish to demand something that your spouse is truly not comfortable giving. While I don't think there's anything wrong with oral sex, for instance, if a spouse really doesn't want to do it, you should never, ever push them. Why would you break trust with someone you love over this? Is it worth wrecking the ability sex has to bring you together? The marriage bed is meant to be an extremely safe place. If you turn it into something that isn't safe because you're insisting on something your spouse doesn't want to do, you're wrecking something precious.

Besides, if it really isn't sinful—or even that extreme—you'll likely find that your spouse will be willing and eager to try it, especially if you spend time being really giving and helping them relax and feel wonderful in bed.

5. Dare yourself. Now for a word to the spouse who isn't as adventurous. I think it's okay to say no to some things you really find distasteful. However, if they're not sinful, I'd encourage you to ask yourself why you think they're distasteful. There may be some ways you can incorporate some of these things into your love life in a non-threatening way, and I'll look at some of them tomorrow.

Some spouses—and let's be honest, it's usually men—do enjoy trying different positions and different things more often than women. This is logical. Women are far more physically vulnerable in sex. Changing positions can be difficult to get used to. Once we find a position that does work for us, with an angle that makes us feel great, we're often less willing to try other things.

It's okay to say no. But then dare yourself to make what you do enjoy absolutely amazing for your spouse! Dare yourself to make sure you really connect on an emotional and spiritual level, too. If you're doing that, and you're making love with regular frequency, you'll likely find that trying some of these other things becomes less of an issue in your marriage, for both of you.

Great Sex Challenge—Day Twenty-Four

Today's challenge actually has three parts!

Part 1: Feel each other's whole bodies. Start at one foot, then go up the side of your spouse's body, touching and licking or squeezing or whatever you want, all the way to the top of the head, and then all the way down the other side. Really see how amazing each of your bodies is.

Part 2: Once you've done that, have an honest discussion about some of the things you'd like to try, you're scared of trying, or that you have already done but really don't like. Some couples find it easier to talk about this with the lights off so they can't see each other's faces, or while spooning so they're not facing each other.

Part 3: At the end, both affirm how much you love and cherish the other—whatever you do in the bedroom. That spiritual connection is always most important!

Day Twenty-Five: Eight Ways to Spice Things Up

For the last two days, we've been talking about stretching the boundaries of what we do during sex—and how we negotiate these boundaries. Today I want to turn this into a more practical, smorgasbord-style post and look at different ways you can become more adventurous in your marriage while still remaining comfortable.

Remember the guidelines we set yesterday, though: no one should ever be pressured to do something they're uncomfortable with or feel is sinful. It is never worth jeopardizing the safety of the marriage bed by pushing something on your spouse!

That being said, sometimes it's not a matter of feeling that it's wrong. More often, we hesitate because:

1. We're a little scared of something new.
2. We think we may not be able to do it right.
3. We're embarrassed.
4. We're afraid that if we try something new, our spouse will want it all the time.
5. We don't think it's sinful, and we don't think it's wrong, it's just not our cup of tea.

Today I am *only* speaking to people in one of those categories. I'm not speaking to anyone who is saying no based on moral reservations or being completely and utterly grossed out. If that describes you, then it is perfectly fine to say no. But again, make sure you're not saying something is morally wrong just because it isn't the missionary position. Sometimes we're too quick to label things as morally wrong (though, of course, some things, like porn, definitely are).

Here are some ideas to help you play games to become more adventurous without violating your sense of decorum.

1. Give "love coupons." Sometimes the idea of having to be at someone's mercy is enticing. We often hesitate sexually because we ask ourselves, "Do I really want to do this? Is this too wild for me?" We get so caught up analyzing it that we're not able to make a decision.

To get around this hesitancy, email your spouse a coupon, saying, "Tonight you own me for an hour" or "Anything you want is yours tonight." If you're going to do this, set up a safe word, like "uncle," that you can say when you feel it's too much. Even if you give coupons, you still have a will and you still have autonomy and can say no.[3]

2. Give each other "veto" chips. At the beginning of the month, each person gets two veto chips, under the following conditions. Throughout the month, when you're making love, you can use a veto chip on something you've already done before. If it's something you've never tried, you can *always* veto it—you don't lose a chip over this. But if you have tried it before, use your chips to veto. And you can't veto a veto!

That way, you each feel as if you're getting your needs met, but you also know you aren't imposing because the other person can say no.

3. Create "his" and "hers" nights. A woman who answered one of my surveys for *The Good Girl's Guide to Great Sex* explained how

3 You can download love coupons at my website (www.sheilawraygregoire.com/freebies/love-coupons).

she and her husband handled this. Her husband tended to be more adventurous than she was, so one evening a week was for him, where they did things that he wanted. Another evening a week was for her, where they did things the way she wanted—like starting with a long back massage and then being very gentle. The other evenings were just "normal." This way, each of them felt that their needs were met and they both went out of their way to make things fun for the other person. After all, they knew it would be reciprocated!

4. Write down fantasies. At the beginning of the year, both of you write down twelve things you would like to do that are special. Maybe you've already done them before, or maybe you haven't. Don't show your spouse what's on your sheet of paper. Fold up the papers and put them in a jar, and once a month, on different nights, each of you draw a piece of paper and do what's on the paper. Again, the rules about saying "uncle" still apply. You never *have* to do anything, but if you each have things written down, and you know it's a give-and-take, then your spouse can feel like you're going out of your way to meet his or her needs without feeling like you have to do it every night. This saves the special things for special nights!

5. Play Match-the-Dice. Get two dice of different colors, and write on a sheet of paper what each dice means. For example, the red dice could be for actions and contain six activities, like kiss, stroke, lick, rub, flick, suck, etc. Each is assigned a number, from one to six. The blue dice could be for different parts of the body. For it, choose six body parts and assign them to one to six, like mouth, fingers, ears, toes, genitals, breasts, etc. Then take turns throwing the dice, and do whatever combination comes up! You can make the game as adventurous or as tame as you want by varying the actions or body parts. Make sure you give enough time—let's say at least a minute—to each task.

6. Play Match-an-Activity. This is a variation on the dice game, but this time, instead of matching an action with a body part, assign a specific activity to each number (either one to six, or one to twelve, depending on how many activities you want to use). Have each of you choose half of the activities that drive you wild. Examples could be mild things, like deep kissing, or blowing and teasing and sucking his ear, to more adventurous things, like watching her rub lotion on her breasts, performing oral sex, or using a specific sexual position. Then get a timer and you must do each thing for two minutes. This constant starting-and-stopping means that you delay orgasm for quite a while, so when it does finally happen it's much more intense.

Sometimes the things we want each other to do stretch our boundaries a bit. So write out your list, with a few extras, and then read your lists together. You can veto ones you're very uncomfortable with, but try to keep at least one that stretches you. If you only have to do it for a maximum of two minutes, that makes it less intimidating while making your spouse feel loved because you're willing to try something new.

7. Create a multisensory experience. We have five senses—sight, sound, touch, taste, and smell. Write down each of the senses on a piece of paper and put them in a jar. Alternate nights, so that you're each responsible for a different night. On your night, pick out three pieces of paper and create a sexual experience that uses all of those senses.

Often we really only use one—touch. We make love with the lights off, we don't say much, and we don't really even taste. Figure out ways to engage the different senses! For sight, she can wear something pretty to bed. For taste, use flavored lip balm, or feed her some chocolate, or whatever you'd like! For hearing, tell her a story. For smell, put on perfume somewhere and ask him to find it. Be creative!

Challenge yourself, though, to come up with different things for each sense when it's your night, so that you're always changing things up a little bit.

8. Play Pick-a-Position. For this one, you'll need a dice and a kitchen timer. Each of you write down your three favorite positions, then assign them to numbers on the dice. If you each pick the same position, add variations to it (like sitting or standing, or in a chair, or legs up or legs down). Then roll the dice and do whatever it says for two minutes, until the timer goes off. Afterward, set the timer for another two minutes and roll the dice.

There you have it—eight ways to try new things and spice things up that are perhaps less intimidating than feeling like you have to always do one particular thing. Sometimes a man (or a woman) will get fixated on one particular sexual thing they want to try. It's okay to say no, but if you regularly do at least one of these ideas, and you make love with relative frequency, you'll likely find that this request becomes less and less important. If you do things slightly differently, your spouse will feel as if your sex life is really exciting, which is what you want—for both of you.

Great Sex Challenge—Day Twenty-Five

Pick one idea and do it! If you're uncomfortable by all of them, start with the dice game and take away the options you're uncomfortable with, replacing them with slightly tamer things. Sometimes just challenging ourselves to try new things helps us see that sex can be a fun celebration we share with one another.

If you're having a lot of fun with this particular challenge, it's okay to make it last several days. Choose one option one night, then try another option the next night. Lather, rinse, repeat!

Days 26–31:

♡

Keep the Momentum Going!

Day Twenty-Six: Deciding on Frequency

We've looked at how to have more fun together, how to see sex in a more positive light, how to make sex feel stupendous, and how to feel intimate. I hope that by this time in the challenge you've experienced some breakthroughs!

However, if you want to keep the momentum going, and keep those breakthroughs coming, you need to set things up so that once this thirty-one-day challenge is over, your intimate life remains a priority. These last few challenges will focus on how to keep these changes alive in your marriage.

When I was writing *The Good Girl's Guide to Great Sex*, I conducted two surveys of over a thousand women each, looking into all kinds of questions, including how much they enjoyed sex, how often they had sex, and how sex had improved since they'd gotten married. I was only planning on interviewing women, but then I started to analyze the results. What floored me was that forty percent of the women reported making love less than once a week.

I decided that I had better survey some guys, too, to find out how they felt about this. The results weren't pretty. I've analyzed the results by age group, religion, and years married, but suffice it to say that there are a lot of rather miserable men. Many women are quite miserable, too, since about twenty-five percent of them reported that their husbands rarely wanted to make love, which made them feel very undesirable.

Making love tells a spouse, "I value you. I love you. I desire you. I accept you." When you don't make love, it's as if you're saying the opposite. That may not seem fair. You think, "Why does everything have to do with sex? Why can't he just love me for who I am?" But men were created to feel affirmation through sex. When we don't want them, they feel as if they aren't loved, even if that's not what we intend. And women were created to feel pursued. If she isn't pursued, she feels as if there's something wrong with her.

I do not believe that women understand how devastating it is to men to be constantly turned down by their wives. Over and over again, I heard men say, "I get rejected so often that I've just stopped asking. It's humiliating."

If you feel like he demands sex too much, you can get mad at him and say that he should just grow up and not need it so much, but then you're imposing your views on him. You're asking him to change, but you're not willing to change. You know something, girls? It really doesn't take much. Just decide to jump in! It doesn't have to take two hours. It likely will take less than half an hour. If you put your mind to it, your body will likely follow. And men, feeling stressed or not feeling in the mood isn't an excuse. Your wife needs to feel connected to you, even if you're tired, overworked, or worried. Put a priority on this if you want to have an intimate, fun, close marriage.

So how often is enough? I would say at least twice a week, if I were forced to pick a number. For some couples, especially when they're younger, more would probably be good. The happiest couples I found were those who were making love three to four times a week. When you connect in that way, it has repercussions on how you feel about each other.

Maybe we should stop asking about the minimum amount of sex we can get away with and start asking, "How can I get in the right frame of mind to show my spouse how much I love him (or her)?" If you make a habit of getting into that frame of mind, I guarantee your marriage will get better!

Great Sex Challenge—Day Twenty-Six

Talk to your spouse about how frequently you each would like to make love. Decide how you're going to come to a compromise which makes you both feel loved and cherished. How can you make this a reality? Does it mean watching less TV at night so you're not tired? How about putting video games aside so you can spend some time with her and make her feel desired? How about making love first thing in the morning?

Figure out what amount is reasonable given your work schedules, kids, and stage of life, and then figure out what practical steps you can take to make that easier to achieve—even if you have to schedule sex!

Heads up: tomorrow's challenge is one that is easier done during the day. Either read the challenge together in the morning, or commit to doing it together the next day.

Day Twenty-Seven: Quickies Can Be Fun!

Today I want to continue talking about frequency by throwing out an idea: **there's nothing wrong with a quickie.**

We've talked about how to spice things up in bed by trying different positions or stretching our comfort zones in safe ways. But there's another way to spice things up, and that's a quickie—a sexual interlude where the goal is usually just to have him reach climax as fast as possible.

I know I've been arguing that sex should be wonderful for both of you, and that it should connect us on a physical, emotional, and spiritual level. How does a quickie fit into that? Doesn't that sound like it's the exact opposite of what I'm talking about?

I don't think so. While I think the sum total of the relationship should be one where you both experience tremendous sexual pleasure, and where you both connect on a profound level, not every single encounter needs to be like that. In fact, having an encounter where you're just laughing (where it's almost like a game) can connect you in a profound way, too. Learning how to play with each other is so important.

So, why a quickie? After all, if women need foreplay to feel good, then quickies won't do much for us, will they? Here are some benefits.

1. You laugh. If you've ever run upstairs while the kids are in front of a DVD, knowing you have very little time, then you know it's funny. You finish, go back downstairs, and pretend like nothing happened. You both share a little secret now.

2. She sees how much he wants her. Ladies, do you feel insecure about your bodies? Do you feel like you're not really attractive? A quickie is often the cure. Most men go to great lengths to make themselves last while you're making love, because they want you to have a good time. But tell him to go as fast as he can because you have to beat the clock, the DVD, the school bus, or whatever it might be, and suddenly you see how much he really does love and desire you. It can be a big ego boost—and that ego boost is also an aphrodisiac, since a large part of the female libido depends on feeling desired.

3. She boosts her libido while calming his down. If it's often been a problem in your relationship that he can't last long enough for her to get real satisfaction, this can be the cure! If you have a quickie early in the day, he satisfies the physical buildup he's feeling, but she rarely does (some women, of course, do find quickies satisfying, but that's the minority). Instead, she starts her libido charging. The next time you make love, he's more likely to last longer, and she's more likely not to take as long.

4. You add variety. It's always good to do things differently sometimes. It shows both of you that you care about the relationship and that you want to keep it fun.

5. You lower his stress. Because many men are worried about their wives receiving pleasure, they often don't get to relax during an encounter. A quickie lets them just focus on the pleasure, which can be very intense.

6. You lower her stress. Men aren't the only ones who get nervous about women receiving pleasure. We women often get quite nervous about it, too, especially if we're trying to orgasm. Take the pressure off, and ironically a quickie can be *very* pleasurable for many women! (Which just shows that we really have to help ourselves relax and focus on pleasure rather than goals.)

So, how does a quickie work best?

Grab five minutes–any five minutes. If he's stressed about work, try a quickie right before he leaves. Or maybe right when he gets home, or right before you head out for a date night.

Have lubricant on hand. Quickies are no fun if you're not lubricated, so here's where Astroglide or K-Y Jelly can help.

Just go with it. Don't worry about doing it right. Just laugh through it! You'll feel emotionally closer because you've shared the experience. And you'll both feel desired.

Great Sex Challenge—Day Twenty-Seven

I'm directing this one at the ladies, since it usually works best if she initiates quickies, especially if you're just starting with them. Grab him during the day, when he's least expecting it, and take him upstairs! This one can be hard to do if you're reading this at night together, so save this challenge until a time when you can actually do it spontaneously. Try to incorporate quickies into your life more often!

Day Twenty-Eight: Why You've Got to Initiate

Today, I want to continue our discussion about how to make sex something that unites you rather than something that drives a wedge between you. Let's talk about an issue that I've touched on a number of times already in this book.

What really matters in a marriage is not so much the frequency of sex (though that is important) as the enthusiasm and passion. So much of a man's self-esteem is tied into whether or not his wife desires him sexually. It's not just that she'll acquiesce to have sex with him; it's that she actually wants to. In fact, if a woman decides to placate her husband and "lie there and think of England," so to speak, he'll experience that as rejection, even though she's "letting him." For many men, that actually leads to erectile dysfunction. They have a difficult time "completing the deed" if they feel like she isn't really there for it.

Now, women who are married to men who don't have high sex drives have problems in this area, too, though it often manifests in slightly different ways. The message to take home is this: your spouse needs to feel like you actually desire and want sex, and not just that you are willing to go through the motions. You've already talked to your spouse about how frequently you're hoping to make love, but it isn't enough to just say, "Okay, we can if you want." You have to show your spouse that you're truly interested.

Many women complain that when they start "letting" him make love more frequently, he gets more demanding. So they just give up. They think, "I'll never satisfy him, so why bother?" The problem is that you haven't met his basic need, which is to feel desired. In fact, if you just lie there and don't really participate, you've reinforced the idea that you don't enjoy sex and don't want to do it. That's going to cause him to desperately want to make sure you do desire him, so he will actually become more urgent about wanting sex. His most basic need, you see, is not to have sex; it's to feel wanted.

At this point, some women are just about ready to give up. Perhaps you ask, "So it's not enough that I have sex? I actually have to want it? How can I force myself to want it?"

Allow me to give you an idea. *Initiate it.* Really. You be the one to give him a big kiss and say, "Let's go upstairs." Take him by the hand after you watch a movie together and lead him to the bedroom. You start the whole process, rather than waiting to see if your spouse is "going to want to tonight."

What's in it for you, you ask? Here are just a few benefits:

1. You have more control over what you do. We talked earlier about how important angle and foreplay is to women. If you initiate, you can take more care that you get the right position and attention you need.

Also, if you're uncomfortable about certain acts (or even uncomfortable about certain parts of your body), you can steer sex in a more comfortable direction for you.

2. You throw yourself into it. You're automatically more active and engaged, and that often means your body will follow more readily.

3. You create a goodwill circle. When you initiate, you show your spouse that you really do desire him (or her). That makes your spouse feel better about you and about the relationship. It's going to make both of you feel closer to each other.

In a marriage, if one person does all the initiating, you have a problem. That person, whether male or female, will feel as if the other spouse doesn't really desire that kind of intimacy, and that's a very lonely feeling.

If you know you're likely going to make love anyway, why not make the extra effort—and it really takes so little effort—to be the one to suggest it, or to try to seduce your spouse? When it's a two-way street, you each feel desired, you each feel loved, and you each feel close to the other. When one does all the asking, it's humiliating. They feel as if their spouse doesn't really love or value being close. They feel as if they're constantly begging. Eventually, as some survey respondents told me, they stop asking, bringing sex to a standstill.

In a healthy relationship, both initiate. If you're in a situation where one spouse initiates eighty to ninety percent of the time, you have an imbalance that can cause problems. One spouse should back off a bit, but the other spouse also needs to fill in those gaps.

So, take a deep breath, take your spouse's hand, and say, "Let's do it!" That one little change can make such a tremendous difference in your marriage.

Great Sex Challenge—Day Twenty-Eight

Without showing your spouse, write down how many times, out of ten, you initiate, how many times your spouse initiates, and how many times it's mutual. Then compare notes. Do you agree? Does one of you obviously initiate more than the other? Talk to each other about how this makes you feel. Then ask each other, "What would be a good way to initiate? What would be fun for you?" See how many ideas you can each come up with! Now, for the lower-desire spouse, pick one and do it!

Day Twenty-Nine: Keeping Your Bedroom Inviting

When my children were babies, my husband and I were living in a tiny two-bedroom apartment. Our computer was in our bedroom. Our duvet was old and rather ugly. In fact, everything in that room was old and ugly.

One winter, after a particularly grueling year during which we were grieving the loss of our little boy, we decided to head south for a vacation and recoup. When we returned home, my mother and a friend had redone our bedroom, with new bedding, plump new pillows, and a new lamp.

Unfortunately, they couldn't move the computer and all the excess stuff out of our room, but even the small effort they made created such a transformation. When I walked into our bedroom, I wasn't depressed anymore. I was happy!

If you're going to keep the changes in your sex life moving forward, you need to have a fun place to connect, and that means having an inviting bedroom. If your dresser is covered with old Visa receipts, if craft boxes are stacked up in a corner, if your bedding is threadbare and ugly and your pillows are lumpy, then climbing into bed isn't fun.

We tend to make it a priority to keep our kitchens and living rooms clean, because that's what other people see when they come into our homes (though, if we're honest, many of us rarely have company). But the bedroom is just for us, so if it's a mess, no one ever sees it.

I remember babysitting for a couple when I was fourteen years old. They had four children in three different bedrooms. Their house was fairly tidy, if loud and chaotic. One night, a toddler wandered into her parents' bedroom, and I followed to corral her back to the rest of us. I was astounded by what I saw. Mountains of clothes were on the floor. Every drawer was open, with clothing hanging out. The bed was a mess and covered with papers. It looked like a cyclone had hit it, unlike the rest of the house.

Twenty-eight years have passed since that day, but I found out just two weeks ago through the grapevine that this couple just divorced. I'm sure that's not the main cause, but it can't have helped. If you're scared to step into your bedroom because it's a mess, or if it's just so ugly that you sigh when you walk in, then it's time to change things!

Messes and laundry aren't the only things that can make our bedrooms unromantic. What about computers and televisions? Bring a screen into the bedroom, and you're likely to stare at it rather than your spouse. Instead of talking and snuggling, you'll catch the ending of *CSI*. That's hardly conducive to romance.

Work isn't all that romantic, either. Flipping through files in bed doesn't help you in the relationship department.

Let's try to banish screens, mess, and work from the bedroom. Let's keep the bedroom an inviting oasis, away from the rest of the world. Let it be a haven where you can escape, just the two of you.

Great Sex Challenge—Day Twenty-Nine

Look around your bedroom. Is it inviting? Why or why not? Do you have a TV in the bedroom? Do you often bring computers or smart phones in? What about work? Discuss with each other how that makes you feel and what you would each like your bedroom to feel like.

How can you bring peace and fun to your bedroom? Do you need new bedding? New rules about what is allowed in?

Once you've decided what you'd like to do, make a date to actually do it. If your bedroom needs to be cleaned up, set the date by which that will be done. If you need to buy new bedding or new pillows, decide when you're going to do that. Put it in the calendar so it will get done. Spending money on your bedroom isn't a selfish extravagance; the best thing you can do for your family is to build a strong marriage. Prioritize that, and everything else falls into place.

Day Thirty: Sex After Parenthood

Sex is obviously the start of parenthood, but for many couples, parenthood is the end of sex. How can you keep your sex life fresh when kids are hanging off you, you're exhausted, and you need time to yourself? For the last twenty-nine days, you've been concentrating on sex, making it a priority. But for these new habits to become "sticky," you have to change your patterns so the roadblocks to a healthy sex life are minimized. For those of us with kids at home, parenting can be one of the biggest roadblocks.

Today's challenge is designed for those with children of any age at home. If you don't have kids at home, you can skip ahead. If your parenting days are still ahead of you, read on so you can plan now about how you want to handle these challenges.

Prioritize Marriage

When I speak at women's conferences, I often ask, "Are you a better wife or a better mom?" Around eighty percent of the average room believes they are better moms. It makes sense. These little beings need us so much, and we love them so much. Children quickly snatch the vast majority of our energy. Our husbands get the leftovers. Men, too, can pour so much into their kids that there's little left for their wives.

Once you have children, though, your marriage is even more important, not less. Other people are counting on you two being rock solid together. You are the foundation for their little lives. You owe it to each other and to your children to put the marriage before the kids.

You can probably all think of couples who prioritized the kids and ignored the marriage relationship. How did that turn out for them? Don't do that. Your children don't need all of your energy all the time. You need to be replenished, and a great way to do that is to build a great marriage.

Keep the Bedroom Safe

If you're going to build a great marriage, you need a safe place in the house when you can be alone, just the two of you.

When my youngest daughter was six, my husband and I were once both enjoying a rather good time in bed when we heard that familiar pitter-patter down the hall. We froze, pulled up the sheets, and were grateful when she jiggled the doorknob and realized it was locked. "It's okay!" she yelled, and we heard her go back down the hall. Relieved, we resumed, until about three minutes later the door burst open and the flurry of sheets began again. It turns out that six is old enough to know how to pick a lock, but not old enough to know that you don't want to be picking that lock.

Keep a good lock on your bedroom door!

The problems, however, don't end when the children get older. Life with teenagers is often even more trying, because teens tend to stay up much later than you do. And they know what's going on.

One friend shared her teen story with me. She and her husband had been enjoying a good time, and when it was over they were lying in bed talking. But their daughter's music was so loud they couldn't hear each other. He got out of bed, opened the door, and yelled, "Jen, how many times do I have to tell you to turn that music down?" She yelled back, "Dad, it's this loud for a reason! Ick!"

You need a safe place for the two of you. One couple I know told their teenagers, "You want to be in your room at 9:00 p.m. I don't care what you do after that, but you don't want to be wandering the halls." The kids got the message, and they cooperated. As much as we may be embarrassed by our kids knowing what we're doing, it actually models a healthy relationship. And it gives them a sense of stability.

My husband and I have encouraged our own girls to be gone the same night of the week to give ourselves a "date night" at home. They both work part-time jobs with similar shifts, and they both go to youth group together.

Don't stop your sex life because you're embarrassed of what the kids may hear. Learn to be silent if you need to. Turn the radio on to muffle the noise if you need to. Most of all, remember that your marriage comes first. Children will not be scarred by learning that their parents are still hot for each other.

Keep the Bedroom Kid-Free

If you have small children, I'd recommend keeping the bedroom kid-free. When babies are first born, pediatricians recommend sleeping them in a bassinet or crib beside your bed. But as they grow, I believe it's best to move children into their own rooms, certainly by six months of age. Children can learn to sleep through the night at that age, and learning to self-soothe is an important skill that gives them security.

I know not all parents agree on this, and many families swear by the "co-sleeping" arrangement where babies and toddlers pile in the bed with their parents. If that's what you both agree is best, that is your prerogative.

I would like to offer a few warnings, however.

First, quite often one spouse is committed to this arrangement while the other is not. That's not fair. If one spouse really wants the bedroom for the couple, that desire matters.

The second caveat is that it's very difficult to have an active, healthy sex life when children are in the bed. Some moms have said to me in frustration, "Sheila, you don't need to have sex in the bedroom! We just make it a point of having great sex elsewhere in the house!" That's wonderful. But here's the thing: often couples start making love when they didn't plan on it beforehand because they're lying in bed just talking, and things happen. If you have kids in bed with you, that easy, low-key spontaneity is gone. Anytime you put up a barrier for something, you make it less likely to occur.

This doesn't mean you can't have a great sex life if your kids sleep with you. It simply means that you'll never have as good a sex life as you could if your kids were out of the bed. Please, think carefully about your marriage before you decide to let the children sleep with you with no end in sight. If you're at the point where you'd like to get them out of the bed, but you don't know how, buy some books on how to help children develop good sleep habits. There are some wonderful ones available, and the techniques do work!

Set Up "Couple Time" Evenings - Or Mornings

Carving out time as parents when you can just be a couple is vital. Schedule this regularly, to help ensure that it happens. When kids know to expect it, it's not a big deal.

Set up once a week "couple evenings" where the children eat a hurried dinner and then play in their rooms, leaving time for you to have a more relaxed dinner, just the two of you. Or set up time on Saturday mornings, when the kids can watch as much TV as they want for a few hours, leaving you the opportunity to stay with each other. Find time that is yours, when the kids know to expect it.

Great Sex Challenge—Day Thirty

Have an honest talk with each other about how much the kids are hampering your sex life. Commit together that your marriage comes first, and figure out ways to find alone time, no matter the ages of the kids. Ask each other, "Do you think I put too much emphasis on the kids, and not enough on you?" Listen humbly to the answer. Then brainstorm together, "How can we carve out couple time? How can we make our bedroom a safe place for us?" Identify some concrete steps you can take to keep your couple time sacred and safe.

Day Thirty-One: Celebrate

You're at the last day of our thirty-one-day challenge! I hope you've found it helpful in opening the lines of communication, discovering new things about your spouse (and yourself), and reaching new fireworks.

On this, our last day, I want you both to celebrate your relationship and how far you've traveled together. I invite you to look forward, not backwards. That mindset is key if the growth and success you've experienced so far is to continue.

Imagine this scenario. A wife realizes that throughout her marriage, she hasn't been sexually generous with her husband. She wants things to be different. At the same time, he's been withholding affection because he doesn't feel loved. They both confess this to each other and resolve to go forward together. They're excited about it!

For a few nights, things go wonderfully. But then, one night, she's extra tired and has a headache. She wants to just go to sleep. He thinks to himself, *Oh, great, here we go again. She said she wanted to change, but she won't. It will never last.* So he gets angry. She knows he's angry, and she thinks to herself, *He doesn't care what I've done all week. That really is all he thinks about!* Before long, they're back to old patterns.

Don't let that be your story! If your spouse has said he or she wants to change, from that time forward commit to seeing your spouse through these new lenses, not your old ones. If she's says she wants to change, and she is changing, then a few nights when she has a headache shouldn't really be a big deal. But if you're obsessing on the past, they will be.

Perhaps you've always doubted whether or not your wife really wants you. Perhaps you've always doubted whether or not he loves you. Perhaps you've always doubted whether or not he's still thinking about porn, not about you. You have to put these worries behind you. If your spouse says he or she wants a new start, believe it! You had a reset button on your intimate life this month. Use it and keep walking forward.

Walking forward is easier to do if you actually change your patterns. Remember way back at the beginning of the thirty-one days, when I suggested learning how to reawaken your body and rediscover each other? That's a wonderful exercise to do every so often. When you're starting again, do it *very* often! It helps you to discover new things, yes, but it also prevents you from doing the "typical"—either rushing through sex or touching each other in ways that perhaps you thought were pleasurable but which really aren't. Reacquainting yourselves with each other's bodies, as if you're doing so for the first time, helps you to trust each other and try something new.

Then do new things! If you tend to make love in a certain way, try something else. Use a different position, a different room, even a different time of day. Just change things up for a while so it feels different and you don't start assuming bad motives of the other. When there has been hurt or distrust, it's difficult to put that behind you. Decide to walk forward in a different way now, with a different outlook.

You've learned some new things this month. You've had some great experiences. Perhaps one of the most important elements is that you've talked together about things that are very important. Carry that forward. So tonight, in our challenge, celebrate how far you've come, what you've enjoyed, and plan to keep moving forward.

First, the practical side of the challenge. What are two or three small things you can put in place to make sure you don't lose the momentum you've built? Maybe they're habits like getting the TV out of the bedroom or going for a walk after dinner. Perhaps it's adopting the "Rule of 3" with positions, where you change things up at least every third time. Write down your ideas and share them with each other.

Now, the romantic side. Write a letter to your spouse, in detail, covering these four areas:

- Here's what I love about sex with you.
- Here's the most sexy thing I think we did this month.
- Here's when I felt closest to you this month.
- Here's what I'm looking forward to in our sex life.

Share those with each other. Writing them down has the benefit of allowing you to save it and look at it again later. If you're not a writing person, talk through the questions. But remember, extra effort always pays off!

My Last Word

I'm so glad you embarked on this journey. My passion is to see marriages thrive so that families and communities can thrive, too. Sex is at the center of all that. We express true intimacy best when our sex lives are healthy, intimate, and exciting. That's how we were made. I pray that this has been a positive experience in your marriage, and I pray that your marriage will only grow stronger from here!

SHEILA WRAY GREGOIRE

the good girl's guide to great sex

(and you thought bad girls have all the fun)

FOREWORD by PAM FARREL

Other Books by Sheila Wray Gregoire

The Good Girl's Guide to Great Sex

Billions of people have had sex. Far fewer have made love. In *The Good Girl's Guide to Great Sex,* author Sheila Wray Gregoire helps women see how sexual intimacy was designed to be physically stupendous but also incredibly intimate.

Whether you're about to walk down the aisle or you've been married for decades, *The Good Girl's Guide to Great Sex* will lead you on a wonderful journey of discovery towards the amazing sex life God designed you for.

With humor, research, and lots of anecdotes, author Sheila Wray Gregoire helps women see how our culture's version of sex, which concentrates on the physical above all else, makes sex shallow. God, on the other hand, intended sex to unite us physically, emotionally, and spiritually. Gregoire walks through these three aspects of sex, showing how to make each amazing, and how to overcome the roadblocks in each area we often encounter.

Drawing on survey results from over two thousand people, she also includes lots of voices from other Good Girls, giving insight into how other women have learned to truly enjoy sex in marriage.

About the Author

Sheila Wray Gregoire speaks around North America, teaching women how to create relationships that thrive. An author of seven books and a syndicated parenting columnist, she started writing when her children were young and she wanted something to do from home. Growing up in a single-parent home gave her a passion to see marriages succeed, and together with her husband, Keith, she speaks at FamilyLife marriage conferences and other marriage outreaches. She also is a sought-after keynote speaker for women's events.

When she's not writing and speaking, you can find her at home in Belleville, Ontario, where she homeschools her two teenage daughters, and she knits. Even in line at the grocery store.

Find her at:

Blog: www.tolovehonorandvacuum.com
Facebook: www.facebook.com/sheila.gregoire.books
Twitter: www.twitter.com/sheilagregoire
Pinterest: www.pinterest.com/sheilagregoire
YouTube: www.youtube.com/sheilagregoire